National Vocational Qualifications
and Further Education

)1

National Vocational Qualifications

AND FURTHER EDUCATION

Edited by **Mike Bees and Madeleine Swords**

**KOGAN
PAGE**

Published in association with the

NC VQ National Council for Vocational Qualifications

© NCVQ, 1990

First published in 1990 by Kogan Page Ltd,
120 Pentonville Road, London N1 9JN

Typeset by DP Photosetting, Aylesbury, Bucks
Printed and bound in Great Britain by
Richard Clay, Bungay

British Library Cataloguing in Publication Data

A CIP catalogue record for this book is available from the British Library

ISBN 0-7494-0245-8

Contents

Introduction

The development and implementation of National Vocational Qualifications, will have a profound effect on colleges of further education. As with any industry in times of change, the most successful organisations are those that seek to actively manage change rather than simply respond to it. Pioneering colleges who anticipated the potential of the 'NVQ revolution', recognise the need to become learner-centred, achievement-led organisations. All aspects of college life must be re-examined, including learning design and delivery: staff development needs will also be of paramount importance.

This anthology draws from the experiences of practitioners in the forefront of these new developments. We address issues that will interest college managers, tutors and employers alike, such as managing change, enhancing employer support and implementing flexible delivery.

In Part 1, 'Embedding NVQs', NVCQ's Director of Research, Development and Information, Gilbert Jessup highlights the significant developments which have led to the present arrangements and future plans for vocational education and training (VET) in the UK. Mr Jessup sets the scene by providing an overview of 'the main features of the emerging model of vocational education and training' and shows how NVQs, the National Record and the NCVQ Database can work together to provide a system that recognises achievement and encourages learning.

Wirral Metropolitan College is a working model of a college in transition. It is committed to extensive changes in all aspects of college life to achieve more effective ways of meeting students' learning needs. Principal Jenny Shackleton's account is essential reading for anyone engaged in making the changes entailed in the delivery of NVQs.

Ernest Theodossin, Deputy Director of The Responsive College Programme, takes a searching look at the gap between what more adult and sophisticated students will expect from FE colleges and the 'user-unfriendly' environments and practices offered by some colleges. Drawing on his experiences here, in the USA and in Europe, he offers constructive guidance for organisations keen to adapt.

The emphasis placed by NCVQ on the demonstration of competence, makes it essential that the traditional links between industry and FE colleges are strengthened to provide access to a wider range of learning and assessment opportunities. Part 2 looks at the 'New deals for employers' that colleges can offer within the new system.

Michael Rowarth, Principal of Newcastle College and a member of the National Task Force for the Training and Enterprise Councils (TECs), gives valuable insights into their workings and advice to colleges on how best to establish a working relationship with their local TEC early on.

Lester Greenacre of the Construction Industry Training Board, describes the NVQ development work of the CITB and argues that a system focused on competence will create greater coherence within VET. He also outlines what CITB hope to achieve from continued collaboration with FE colleges. John Millington, Engineering ITB and former member of the HMI, stresses the importance of NCVQ's broad definition of competence: 'competence means more than training and more than education . . . as they have been known in the past.' He analyses the way employers in the engineering industry are responding to the challenges of NVQs and looks to a possible future 'entrepreneurial role' for colleges in providing learning and assessment opportunities for NVQs.

In Part 3, 'Implementing flexible delivery', the possibilities of an NVQ-led model of learning and assessment are addressed. Increasingly learner-centred styles of delivery create a need for different systems of learner support and guidance. Within the Newham Community College model, guidance is taken as the context for learning/teaching rather than something that has been grafted onto provision. The authors argue that guidance should be explicitly built into all stages of the learning, ie at selection, induction, during delivery, and during transition phases. The optimal location of this guidance is also something that must be looked at afresh. This chapter provides a good example of how one college has sought to embed within its provision, a heightened awareness of student needs.

Within NVQs, the Accreditation of Prior Learning is a method of assessment that involves identifying acceptable evidence of an individual's past achievements and matching these with the competence requirements of an NVQ. Given the great potential of this route as a means of widening access to qualifications, the APL process is one which is of interest to NCVQ and the Training Agency. A joint national project was set up to examine APL and to identify factors that influence its effectiveness. Newport and Crosskeys College formed part of this and the chapter by John Newman and Nick Llewellin looks at a general model of the APL process and then goes on to outline the college's specific approach to APL.

David Hutchinson, (North Notts College) analyses the benefits of the new system of competence-based qualifications for those with special needs. Hutchinson highlights credit accumulation, alternative modes of assessment and varied learning routes as key factors and gives some guidelines that institutions might consider when reviewing their provision.

Roy Boffy looks at the opportunities offered to colleges in a system where off-the-job training is not the 'only part of the whole learning/ training process which attracts formal accredited recognition'. NVQ-led, work-based learning can contribute to the development of 'effective quality training' in raising the awareness of occupational competence, focusing on individual learning needs, and promote integration within training programmes.

Inevitably with such fundamental issues, there remains much which is left unsaid. Every organisation will, of course, have to develop its own strategies to implement NVQs in the context of local employment needs and changing student profiles. However, we feel that with *National Vocational Qualifications and Further Education*, we have managed to capture some of the best practices within further education today. These are offered as examples rather than as prescriptive models: we are sure that they will interest all those who believe in the future of further education.

Mike Bees
Madeleine Swords

1 May 1990

The views expressed by the authors within this anthology do not necessarily reflect those of the editors, nor of the NCVQ.

Notes on the contributors

Mike Bees. As Principal of North London College Mike Bees played a leading role in the development of vocational and pre-vocational education in the ILEA. For the past two years, on behalf of various National Agencies, he has travelled the country listening and talking to the staff of FE colleges, ET/YT schemes, and employers adjusting to the effects of the implementation of National Vocational Qualifications within their organisations.

In collaboration with **Patricia McQuade**, the other senior partner in TED Consultants, he is currently engaged in developing vocational education and training programmes in Europe, with a special emphasis on France, for employed and unemployed adults from the United Kingdom.

Roy Boffy is currently General Adviser for Further Education with Dudley LEA. Before taking up this post in 1986, he was a Project Leader (Midlands Region) in the ESF/YTS Core Skills Project from 1983–6, based in the Faculty of Education at Wolverhampton Polytechnic. From 1965 to 1983 he taught at Oldbury and Wulfrun Colleges of Further Education. Initially teaching General Studies to Craft and Technician apprentices, he progressed to developing Social and Life Skills provision for YOP trainees and to workplace supervisor training. Previous publications include a series of articles for *NATFHE Journal* on work-based learning and further education (1984–5), an article on the future of General Studies in *JFHE* (1980), and major contributions to MSC and FESC publications, including *Work-based Projects in YTS* (1985), the series of exemplar work-based projects (1985), and *Learning in YTS: Design & Integration Issues*.

Lester Greenacre is Executive Assistant (Special Projects) with the Construction Industry Training Board, a role which currently embraces advising on and co-ordinating work on the emerging NVQ framework and developing the Board's policy on pre-vocational issues, in particular emphasis on curriculum development. Prior to this, he was responsible for Open Learning and the 'Open Learning in Construction' initiative. He is an Educational Technologist, with a background in teaching, and joined CITB in 1979 to research and develop learning and teaching strategies which would assist in improving the overall effectiveness of training in the construction industry.

David Hutchinson, a graduate in psychology and educational management, is Director of Training and Staff Development at the North Nottinghamshire College of Further Education. Since 1970 he has been involved in the education and training of young people with special needs. More recently, he has been extensively involved in staff training and has had a number of books published concerned with curriculum development for young people with special needs and staff training in that field. A member of the Warnock Committee of Enquiry in the Education of Handicapped Children and Young People, David Hutchinson is currently a member of the Further Education Unit's Special Needs Advisory Committee and a Vice-Chair of SKILL – The National Bureau for Students with Disabilities.

Gilbert Jessup is Director of Research, Development and Information for the National Council for Vocational Qualifications. He set up and became the first Director of the Work Research Unit (1974–8) in the Department of Employment, with the remit to improve the quality of working life in British industry. While at the MSC (1982–7), he played a central role in formulating the MSC strategy in developing employment-led standards and assessment methods leading to new forms of modular qualifications. He initiated many of the early development projects in this field and helped to establish competence-based training. He was influential in reshaping the framework of YTS and introducing the Record of Achievement. At the NCVQ (since 1987) he has devised an R&D programme, introduced the National Record of Vocational Achievement (NROVA) and has been influential in developing the NVQ model. Gilbert Jessup was made honorary Professor of Occupational Psychology at Nottingham University in 1976.

Nick Llewellin BA (Hons) Cert Ed Dip Ed is Principal Lecturer at Crosskeys College, a PICKUP Co-ordinator for Gwent and the Project Manager of the joint Crosskeys/Newport APL Project. He is

currently completing a Masters Degree. **John Newman**, BA (Hons)
Cert Ed FMS is Vice Principal of Newport College of Further
Education, a Member of National Council of Association of Vice
Principals and an Executive Member of National Education
Committee of the Institute of Management Services. He is Co-
ordinator of Gwent LEA 5-College ET Training Manager Scheme
and Financial Controller of the APL Crosskeys/Newport Project.

John Millington, CEng, BSc, Eng (Hons), NIME, FRSA, has had
a career in industry and further and higher education. His last colleges
were Garnett College of Education (Senior Lecturer) and Henley
College of Further Education (Head of Department of Engineering).
He was a HMI specialising in manufacturing engineering and further
education staff training in Wales and England, a past member of
Hargreaves Committee of CGLI, an assessor to various CGLI, BTEC
and CNAA committees and boards, and an assessor to the EITB
Training and Education Committee for several years while a HMI.
He joined the EITB as National Education Adviser in 1988.

Aidan Pettitt was formerly a project worker with the TA/FESC
Work Based Learning Project and has undertaken consultancy work
for the FEU on competency-led learning. He is now PL/NVQ Co-
ordinator at Newham Community College. **Geoff Crook** is a SL at
NCC. He is a Centre Co-ordinator for the NCVQ/TA Accreditation
of Prior Learning Project and manages the College Progression
Project. This chapter was developed with the guidance and support of
Ruth Silver, Vice-Principal, Newham Community College.

Michael Rowarth is Principal of Newcastle College, a member of
National Training Task Force and a Board Member of the Tyneside
Training and Enterprise Council. He is the Immediate Past President
of the Association for College Management, Past President of the
Association of College Principles and a Member of the Board of
Management of the Further Education Unit. Locally, he is Chairman
of the Management group of the Newcastle Accredited Training
Centre, a member of the Boards of the Regional Management Centre
and the Newcastle Youth Enterprise Centre. Educated at Oxford,
London and Manchester Universities, Michael Rowarth spent some
time in schools before moving into Further Education. He then spent
five years in training with the Burton Group before returning to
Further Education. He has been Principal at Newcastle College since
1979.

Jenny Shackleton is Principal of the Wirral Metropolitan College, a large (Group 10) locally maintained college largely offering non-advanced further education to the Wirral and North Cheshire. Before joining that College she was the Senior Assistant Education Officer (MSC Co-ordinator) for Bedfordshire between 1983 and 1987. That post followed various college and training centre management posts in Bedfordshire. Jenny Shackleton has worked closely with the Training Agency/MSC and other national and government organisations (such as FEU and FESC) since the mid-1970s, particularly in the role of adviser, consultant, and manager of numerous projects. She is currently a member of the Lead Industry Body for Administrative, Business and Commercial Occupations, and of the Post Network.

Madeleine Swords is a Development Officer with the NCVQ, her main area of responsibility being the development and implementation of the National Record of Vocational Achievement and associated products and services. She has a degree in Occupational Psychology and an MBA.

Ernest Theodossin was born and educated to BA level (University of Michigan) in the United States. He came to Britain as a postgraduate student, received an MA from the University of London, taught English (school, technical college, college of education) and became a naturalised British subject. In the 1970s he retrained in education management, was awarded a PhD by the University of London Institute of Education for work in planned change, and taught (institute of higher education, university) in this field before joining the Further Education Staff College (FESC) as a staff tutor in 1981. From 1985 to 1989 he was Deputy Director of the Responsive College Programme, a joint FESC-Manpower Services Commission college marketing project which carried out developmental work in England, Scotland and Wales. In 1989 he was invited to Australia on a Commonwealth Visiting Fellowship. He is presently undertaking work for the establishment of a national support agency to assist colleges with marketing and promotion. For FESC he has published *Management Restructuring in a FE College* (1984), *The Modular Market, In Search of the Responsive College* (both 1986), and *The Responsive College* (1989), currently the major British work on college marketing, which brings together the results of 21 projects involving more than 50 colleges.

Part 1: Embedding NVQs – managing change

1. National Vocational Qualifications: implications for further education

Gilbert Jessup

INTRODUCTION

A variety of national initiatives and developments have taken place throughout the 1980s to improve and extend Vocational Education and Training (VET) in the UK. Their impact has been felt in schools, further education and in industry. From what appeared to be a variety of ad hoc initiatives to meet specific concerns (eg raising educational standards, skill shortages, unemployment) a pattern is now emerging which it is hoped will provide a coherent model of development and progress in the 1990s.

The main characteristics of the new model were presented in *A New Training Initiative (NTI)*, published as long ago as 1981[1]. This set out the objectives to be achieved if the UK was to meet its training needs in a rapidly changing and increasingly competitive economic environment. A key feature of this publication was the introduction of a new concept of 'standards', although its significance was little understood by readers in 1981. In fact the key sentence was tucked away in the middle of the document (page 6, paragraph 19): 'at the heart of this initiative lie standards of a new kind.'

In this chapter I shall indicate the main features of the emerging model of VET, with specific reference to the qualification system which will provide the structure in which vocational education and training will operate. It will be evident that the standards-based qualifications that are now being created will play a more significant role in shaping education and training than did the traditional, norm-referenced qualifications which were common in the past.

The shift is from a system that was largely defined in terms of its inputs to one defined by its outputs. By inputs, we mean the syllabuses, the courses or the training programmes, ie the specification of the learning opportunities provided. By output we mean the 'standards' that need to be achieved at the end of a learning programme. 'Standards' is a shorthand term used to describe a clear specification of the performance required of an individual, and this includes the level or standard of performance. As we shall see this is set out in a 'statement of competence'. The term 'standards' in the new model thus has a specific meaning, unlike the generalised and rather loose concept of standards which has prevailed in educational circles in the past. These new standards will be 'packaged' as qualifications and units of credit. To determine whether an individual has achieved a standard one needs some form of assessment. A qualification is a record of this achievement.

The shift to an output-led system of education and training thus means a qualification-led system. This statement makes many people unhappy because they think of qualifications as 'sitting exams' and writing essays or doing multiple-choice tests. If this were the case I would share their concern. Educationalists are also made unhappy by the statement because they believe that qualifications do not and can not assess many of the finer aspects of the learning that they believe to be important. They are right if they think only in terms of traditional forms of qualifications. But this is not what we are now talking about.

Along with the new standards must go new forms of assessment, very different from sitting examinations. The model only works if assessment can cover all the things we want people to learn (and, more important, what the learner wants to learn). It also only works if assessment is more friendly and facilitates learning rather than acting as a deterrent or just an obstacle to be overcome. We are therefore talking not only about new kinds of standards and new forms of assessment, but also about new forms of learning. People will no doubt object to this statement, for nothing is ever new. But let us say that these features are not common and in the past have not been normal practice in education or training. The other aspect is how the standards, assessment and learning, and the other features we shall be describing, relate to each other. This is what we mean by a model. The overall package is new. This chapter describes the characteristics of the new model.

The Review of Vocational Qualifications

A significant step towards the new VET model was made by the Review of Vocational Qualifications carried out by a working group set up by the government in April 1985[2] and which reported in 1986.[3] It recommended: the development of standards, picking up the NTI concept; new forms of qualifications, to be described as National Vocational Qualifications (NVQs); and the creation of a new framework for such qualifications, the NVQ framework. It also recommended the setting up of a new body to carry through these proposals, the National Council for Vocational Qualifications. These proposals were endorsed in a government White Paper *Education and Training - Working Together*, 1986.[4]

Criteria have been set to show the standards qualifications are required to meet if they are to be incorporated in the national framework. The criteria for National Vocational Qualifications (NVQs)[5] make many aspects of the proposed model explicit. The 'new kinds of standards' advocated in the New Training Initiative are now being put into operation through the introduction of NVQs.

CONCERNS AND AIMS

The whole of this initiative, from the review of vocational qualifications onwards, has been characterised by the need for great urgency and the setting of highly ambitious targets by the government. This reflects the growing recognition that to succeed economically in an increasingly competitive world, the UK needs to raise significantly the competence of the workforce. Comparisons with our economic competitors show how we lag behind other countries in the standards of education and training achieved, and future projections show that we shall lag even further behind - and behind far more countries - by the end of the century if we do not urgently address this issue. This is why education and training have been moving up the political agenda in recent years.

The issue is not simply that we need more education and training but also that we need a change in kind. Education needs to prepare people more broadly for employment and life in general. Training needs to be less narrow, concentrating more on adaptability and transferability of skills to cope with changing technology, work practices and organisational structures.

Traditional careers, starting with a period of initial training, followed by stable employment within an occupation, are becoming less common. The pattern in the future will be initial training followed by frequent periods of updating and retraining to cope with the changing requirements of employment. A wide range of jobs are being upgraded. Employees need to solve problems rather than just follow procedures and perform routine activities. Employees must look for ways of doing the job better, of improving their efficiency, improving the quality of products they make and services they offer. This has been a feature of life in Japanese companies for some time.

The complementary issue is the recognition that in previous generations the potential of the majority of individuals has seldom been fulfilled through their employment. There is a wealth of untapped human potential which, given the opportunity, could be developed and employed in more creative and satisfying work. One only has to look at the educational levels now achieved and the way people are employed in many other countries to realise what is possible.

The new model is an attempt to meet the needs of both industry and individuals. These needs are not incompatible.

Competence in employment

One of the growing concerns among employers has been that much of the provision of VET was not seen as being directly relevant to needs of employment. Although there were many exceptions, it was considered that VET tended to be 'educationally' orientated both in content and in the values which are implicit in its mode of delivery. It has tended to concentrate on the acquisition of knowledge and theory while neglecting performance, and it is performance which essentially characterises competence.

The educational influence is apparent, for example, in the forms of assessment adopted in vocational qualifications where written and multiple-choice tests carry more weight than practical demonstrations. Assessment practices such as sampling, providing a choice of questions and adopting pass marks of around 50 per cent, are all imports from an educational model of assessment, which have little place in the assessment of competence. Discrimination between individuals tends to guide the design of assessment instruments (norm-referencing) even when the objectives sought are the standards required in employment (criterion-referencing). These practices are of course being questioned in educational qualifications, and the recent introduction of GCSE, and more particularly the National Curriculum which is under development, represent moves towards assessing educational skills and criterion referencing. The effect of this bias has been not only to reduce the relevance of VET to employment but also to exclude large segments of the population who do not find it easy, or have no wish, to learn in an 'academic' environment. The new VET model is designed for the whole population, and not just for the 40 per cent or so who have participated in the past.

The new National Vocational Qualifications are unashamedly

about assessing competence. Occupational competence is about being able to perform in employment. But it is not simply concerned with performance in a particular job, as some have mistakenly interpreted it due to the new emphasis given to assessment at work. Being able to perform effectively in a work role, taking account of all the organisational and interpersonal problems employees have to cope with in their day-to-day work, is certainly at the heart of occupational competence. But an NVQ attests to something beyond this. The award of an NVQ, which we must remember is a national qualification based upon national standards, implies that the holder can perform the functions listed in the NVQ statement of competence in any company or job where they are practised. For example, one would expect a plumber to fit appliances or mend pipes in a wide variety of situations, including those he or she has never before come across. This means that an NVQ needs to assess not only whether a person can perform the functions as they are presented in one job but whether they can also transfer those skills to other jobs. This is why an understanding of the principles underpinning the activities and an awareness of the variations in conditions one might meet is important and should be included in the assessment.

Access

Access was a central issue identified in both the New Training Initiative and the Review of Vocational Qualifications. There appeared to be far too many unnecessary barriers and constraints in gaining entry to VET and gaining qualifications. For example, some courses specified age limits, some specified periods of prior experience, the majority required candidates to undergo a course or programme of training of a certain duration with specified modes of learning at specified institutions. In many occupations it was practically impossible to gain entry if one had not entered training or become apprenticed at a particular age. In many areas, many obviously competent people could not gain formal recognition of their competence because they had not come through the traditional qualification route. Barriers to access have presented particular problems to those with special needs.

The qualification jungle

Yet another problem identified by the Review of Vocational Qualifications was the confusion created by numerous awarding bodies competing in the same or overlapping occupational areas, with qualifications with different objectives, size and structure, often with no procedures for recognising each others' qualifications. This lack of coherence has often created problems in the career progression and mobility of individuals and inefficiencies in the VET provision. Individuals found their career paths blocked or had to embark upon training programmes in areas that they had at least partially covered before. Access to higher education and the professions via vocational routes was also unnecessarily restricted.

The NVQ criteria

The criteria set for NVQs have been formulated in order to overcome the problems identified and meet the objectives outlined above. The new qualifications being developed must meet specified criteria to be accredited as NVQs. These are set out in NVQ Criteria and Procedures.[5] The main features of an NVQ are outlined below.

Statement of competence

NVQs are commonly described as competence-based, which of course they are, but this term can mean many things to different people. The key feature of NVQs is that they are based on an explicit 'statement of competence', and this point needs to be emphasised. The specification has to be written down for everyone to see, in an agreed and recognisable format.

The statement of competence spells out what candidates are required to demonstrate for the award of an NVQ, including the performance criteria against which performance is judged. In doing so, the statement of competence also sets clear goals for education and training programmes. The specification of competence plus the performance criteria provide the operational realisation of the 'new kind of standards' (see Figure 1.1).

Employment-led

The NVQ statements of competence are derived, not from an analysis of education and training programmes, but from an analysis of employment requirements, ie an analysis of the functions employees carry out, paying particular attention to purpose and outcome. In addition, the analysis is carried out by, or on behalf of, employers and employees in the relevant sector and is endorsed by them. Thus the term 'employment-led standards'.

Alternative modes of learning and assessment

Statements of competence derived through this employment-led

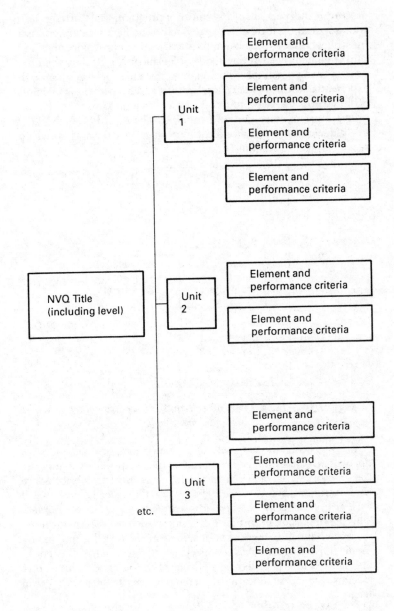

Figure 1.1 *The statement of competence*

process are independent of any course or programme of learning. This is an important feature of NVQs, which embody this statement. As a consequence of this separation from the learning provision, an NVQ can be gained through any mode of learning. NVQs thus open the way to recognition of vocational competence achieved through experiential learning, workplace learning and open learning and puts achievements via these routes on an equal footing to more formal programmes of education and training. The award of an NVQ is solely dependent upon assessed competence, not the way in which such competence is acquired (see Figure 1.2).

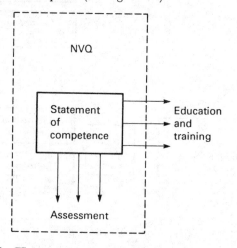

Figure 1.2. *The statement of competence is independent of the mode of assessment and learning*

Less obviously, the statement of competence is also independent of the method of assessment. The nature of the competence will indicate the category of evidence required for assessment (ie performance demonstrations, knowledge, etc) but within that category options will exist as to the specific method or instrument of assessment adopted. This legitimises other forms of assessment such as assessment in the workplace and assessment of prior achievement, as well as recognising more conventional forms of assessment. These are all seen as alternative forms of collecting evidence of competence.[6] This further extends access to qualifications and has relevance to those with special needs.

Unit credits

Another feature of NVQs which has major implications for the way in which education and training is provided, is that the qualifications will consist of a number of units of competence. Each unit, which represents a relatively discrete area of competence with independent value in employment, can be separately assessed and accredited to an individual. This opens the way to the possibility of credit accumulation towards gaining a qualification (see Figure 1.3).

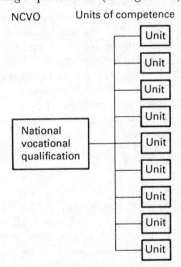

Figure 1.3 *Units of competence*

NCVQ has in fact launched a national system of credit accumulation and transfer based upon such unit credits. The 15 major national awarding bodies offering vocational qualifications within NVQ levels I-IV have agreed to participate and to offer their qualifications in the form of units where they do not already do so. A longer-term goal is the recognition by awarding bodies of each others' units for the purpose of credit accumulation towards qualifications. Rationalisation achieved through adopting agreed national standards (statements of competence) for NVQs will facilitate this process.

To summarise, unit credits and the independence of qualifications (and units) form specific modes of learning, and assessment provides the structures which allow access to qualifications, in a way which has not been possible in the past. To exploit the full potential of NVQs, vocational education and training, or more precisely the provision of learning oppotunities to acquire competence, must be provided in a highly flexible manner. This is currently presenting a considerable challenge to the staff of further education colleges, and those managing training programmes.

THE NVQ FRAMEWORK

The framework is being created by allocating NVQs as they become accredited by NCVQ to an area of competence and a level within a unified national system. The framework has until recently been limited to four levels, spanning qualifications from the most basic to those approximating to Higher National. In February 1989, however, NCVQ was invited by the government to extend the framework to make possible the inclusion of qualifications at 'professional' levels. Following consultations with professional bodies and other interest groups, the framework has recently been extended to include level 5. The government has expressed the intention that the NVQ framework should be comprehensive and include vocational and professional qualifications at all levels.

The purpose of the framework is to facilitate transfer and progression, both within occupational areas and between them. This is being achieved by grouping together those qualifications that are similar in their statements of competence. Through a process of rationalisation, functions which appear in different occupations or industrial sectors (eg cash handling, customer services, reception

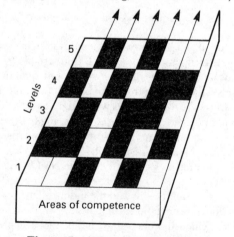

Figure 1.4 *The NVQ framework*

duties) should be expressed in units which are common to those different occupations or industries. Thus qualifications will often share common units, providing indications of routes of progression and transfer between different areas (see Figure 1.4).

Apart from the Lead Industry Bodies (LIBs) which specify the standards in the occupational areas for which they are responsible, a number of 'generic' lead bodies have been set up to create standards in functional areas which are cross-sectorial. The Administrative, Business and Commercial Training Group provided an early example of a cross-sectorial body. More recently groups have been set up to cover management and supervision, information technology, training and development, and foreign languages. Apart from developing NVQs for those specialising in these areas, it is expected that the units specified will be adopted widely and incorporated in NVQs where appropriate across all sectors. Centrally devised units obviously offer maximum potential for rationalisation within the NVQ framework.

The national system of credit accumulation

To take full advantage of the unit structure and unit credit arrangements created by NVQs, the National Council has introduced a national system of credit accumulation. This operates through the National Record of Vocational Achievement (NROVA) which was launched by NCVQ in June 1988 (see Figure 1.5). The 14 major national awarding bodies were invited to participate in the national system at the time it was launched and all agreed to do so. One aspect of this agreement was that they would co-operate in a process of mutually recognising the units offered by the other awarding bodies as contributions to their own qualifications where they met the requirements. In so far as qualifications, within the NVQ framework, will frequently share common units as described above, this will not present any technical problems.

The National Record was initially piloted in a number of colleges and training centres. It is now being adopted more widely, although its full potential will not be realised until the NVQ framework is fully developed and all qualifications are offered in unit form. It has been adopted within the government's training programmes, ET and YTS, so its widescale use is guaranteed. During the first months after its introduction about three-quarters of a million NROVAs were issued.

The National Record is in fact far more than the repository of unit credit certificates and qualifications. It mirrors the model of education and training presented in this chapter. It is designed to contain the

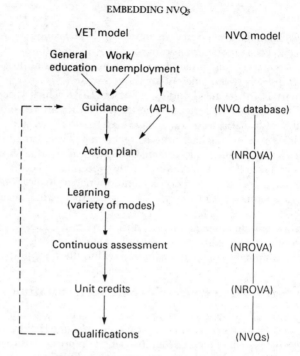

Figure 1.5 *The NVQ model of VET*

Action Plan (see below), the Continuous Assessment Record, the Unit Credit Certificates and the NVQs or other qualifications awarded. The revised version introduced in 1990 extends its use by incorporating an initial section for a summary of the school's record of achievement and basic information on the holder in the form of a CV, should inclusion of these be desired. This addition has been made in response to many requests during the extensive evaluations which have taken place. NCVQ is also exploring with other agencies the potential for extending its use further to align with, or to incorporate, the school's record of achievement when the government's policy on this issue is clarified.

NCVQ database

Another vital tool available to support the implementation of the new VET model is a computerised database. The database, which became publicly available in April 1990, contains detailed information on all NVQs, units and their elements of competence and performance criteria. Related information includes assessment methods and the awarding body for each NVQ and unit. Units and NVQs are classified according to a number of dimensions of competence and linked to the primary occupations where the competence is practised. While the NVQ framework is being established, comparable data will be held, in so far as they are available, on other national qualifications and the emerging specifications of competence from industry.

The data are available via local terminals linked to the database, which enables an interactive user-friendly dialogue. This will greatly enhance counselling, career planning and the design of training programmes. The database will not only allow individuals and their advisers to inspect the national provision of qualifications, but also the competences required in different areas of employment. With sophisticated software it will be possible for an individual to generate a profile of their claimed competence, in the form of units of competence, as a starting point to consideration of how they might progress. From the initial profile, alternative menus could be offered of further qualifications which build upon the individual's current competence in a systematic way.

Building on the above concept, software will be developed for generating action plans, to be used initially in government training programmes, but which have much wider application. The action plans will be printed out directly from the database, in the form of units, elements and performance criteria, and any other information which is required. The print-out is being designed for insertion in the National Record to initiate the training process.

We are also exploring ways in which the qualifications/compe-tence database can be linked to databases of education and training provision (eg TAPs, ECCTIS), so that once an individual has decided what she or he wishes to pursue, further information can be obtained on where or how the relevant learning opportunities and experience are provided.

Generic units and common learning outcomes

An additional concern in establishing the NVQ framework has been the need to link VET more closely to the general education provision. It should be recalled that the White Paper which provided the remit for NCVQ was entitled *Working Together – Education and Training*.[4] One mechanism for achieving this was proposed by Kenneth Baker, when he was Secretary of State for Education, in his speech 'Further Education: A New Strategy', delivered on 15 February 1989.[7] Among a variety of proposals, he suggested introducing a core curriculum that was needed by everybody to cope with life and employment and which should form part of the curriculum, whether young people pursued academic or training (VET) routes after the age of 16 years. This proposal has been taken up by the present education minister, John MacGregor. On 28 November 1989 he wrote to the National Curriculum Council asking them to draw up a framework of core skills which could be incorporated in A/AS level and post-16 education more generally. He also wrote to the Secondary Education and Assessment Council who are responsible for assessment in A/AS levels, as well as GCSE.

The CBI is also promoting this concept and has suggested a set of Common Learning Outcomes, common that is to all education and training provision, possibly from age 14 onwards.[8] Note here the word 'outcomes' rather than curriculum. This is in keeping with the model described in this chapter and, if defined as outcomes, it would allow the common components to be pursued through different forms of learning, such as an academic discipline or an occupation. The CBI also sees the concept of 'generic' units, adopting the methodology of the NVQ units of competence, as a potential method of defining and assessing the Common Learning Outcomes.

The NCVQ worked with the National Curriculum Council to help them formulate their proposals for a set of core skills to be incorporated in A/AS levels. While making A/AS levels more relevant to future employment requirements, the further goal sought by NCVQ is to achieve commonality between educational and vocational qualifications.[9] The model described here could thus be further extended to incorporate unit credits in core aspects of competence such as numeracy, communications and problem-solving, in addition to occupationally related competence as incorporated in NVQs.

Generic units, as part of a life-long credit accumulation system starting in schools, provide an exciting prospect of bringing the academic and VET streams closer together in a way that has not been technically possible in the past. The National Record of Vocational Achievement is also being seen as the potential instrument in which to accumulate such credits in the different programmes and contexts.

THE EMERGING MODEL OF VET

NVQs, the credit accumulation system and the database are collectively designed to provide the structure to meet the perceived needs of vocational education and training in the 1990s and beyond. The features of the model (see Figure 1.5) may be linked in the following sequence:

- a comprehensive provision of competence-based qualifications will be available, relevant to all primary requirements of employment;
- opportunities will be provided for all people post full-time general education to pursue vocational training prior to and during employment;
- educational and career guidance will be available through a variety of agencies and the NVQ framework/database will provide the language and the means to structure such guidance;
- initial assessment and the accreditation of prior learning will provide the baseline of competence for individual action plans;
- individual action/learning plans will be negotiated and drawn up following initial assessment and guidance (action plans form the second part of the National Record);
- vocational education and training will be provided in a variety of forms to suit individual needs and opportunities. The models of learning will include college/training-centre tuition, work-place/work-shop practice, open learning – all available full-time and in combination to suit the individual learner;
- assessment of competence will normally be at unit level;
- assessment will be continuous and unit-credits may be gained when the individual has met the requirements of a unit (record of continuous assessment forms the third part of the National Record);
- individuals will complete programmes of learning and will be awarded the appropriate qualifications (maintained in the National Record);
- the above cycle will be repeated or entered into at various points throughout an individual's career and every encouragement will be given to individuals to continue to learn and update their competence. This will be made easier by virtue of the unit-based credit system and multi-mode learning possibilities to meet individual needs.

The above model of education and training implies that colleges and training centres move towards acting in the capacity of learning resource and assessment centres, providing a variety of opportunity for individuals to learn. It is based on the perceived needs of individuals, employers and the economy. The extent to which education and training providers can meet such needs, and at what cost, is beginning to be explored through a variety of institutional development programmes.

APPENDIX

Research and development issues

The current programme to institute the model, as one might expect, is throwing up a range of technical issues in respect of competence specification, assessments, learning and transfer on the one hand, and institutional and staff development on the other. While a programme of research and development has been building up over the last few years, mainly funded through the Training Agency and more recently NCVQ, and experience is accumulating, many issues remain unresolved or in need of refinement. The following list attempts to identify some of the most salient that are exercising researchers working in the programme at present.

1 There is continuing debate on an appropriate concept of 'competence'. Competence is conceived as being much broader than specifications of skill that have existed in traditional training programmes. Competence should incorporate all that is required to perform effectively in employment, which includes managing the competing demands within a work role, interpersonal relationships and so on. The Mansfield-Mathews Job Competence Model[10] perhaps comes closest to what researchers currently seek but it needs considerable refinement. In particular, competence should incorporate the ability to respond flexibly and adapt to changing situations.

2 Making the concept of competence work within a 'statement of competence' gets to the heart of the model and while experience in the area is growing, the principles and methods governing such statements need to be clearly articulated. The programme will succeed or fail depending on how well this objective can be achieved.

3 In particular, the role of 'knowledge and understanding', and more generally the cognitive components of competence, within the statement of competence are currently a major issue of debate and the subject of a number of research initiatives.

4 A new model of assessment is being developed, where assessment is related directly to the elements of competence and 'sufficiency of evidence' is the key concept.[6] The model needs extensive evaluation.

5 Assessment in the workplace and a variety of forms of competency testing are being developed and evaluated. Assessment based on evidence of prior achievements (commonly presented

under the 'accreditation of prior learning' label) is being researched in major national projects.[11]

6 The role of 'generic' competences, that is those which are common to a wide range of occupations and activities, including the underpinning core competences of number, communications, problem-solving, etc, is the major new issue for research. The issue has recently excited politicians and employers, who perceive generic units as a way of developing coherence between general and vocational education. The National Record of Vocational Achievement is also seen as an instrument to bridge the education/vocational divide.

7 Returning to the concept of competence and the components of competence (skill, knowledge, understanding, etc), fundamental questions are being asked afresh on the process of learning itself and the generalisability, or transferability, of competence from the place of learning to other contexts.

8 The need to be explicit about what is learnt and assessed within the emerging model of VET raises fundamental issues which in traditional models of education are perhaps assumed without question and seldom raised.

REFERENCES

1 *A New Training Initiative: An Agenda*, MSC, December 1981.
2 *Education and Training for Young People*, HMSO, March 1985.
3 *Review of Vocational Qualifications in England and Wales: A Report by the Working Group*, MSC/Department of Education and Science, April 1986.
4 *Working Together – Education and Training* (Cmnd 9823), July 1986.
5 *The NVQ Criteria and Procedures*, NCVQ, March 1989.
6 See *NCVQ Information Note 4: Assessment in National Vocational Qualifications*, November 1988.
7 'Further Education: A New Strategy', Speech by the Rt Hon. Kenneth Baker MP, DES, D/d 8051748, 1989.
8 See recommendations in *Towards a Skills Revolution*, CBI, October 1989.
9 *Common Learning Outcomes: Core Skills in A/AS levels and NVQs*, NCVQ, R & D Report No. 6, April 1990.
10 *Job Competence – a description for use in vocational education and training*, Further Education Staff College, 1985.
11 See *NCVQ Information Note 5: Assessment in NVQs: Use of Evidence from Prior Achievement ('APL')*, January 1989.

2. NVQs: A whole college approach

Jenny Shackleton

INTRODUCTION

For many of us working in and for colleges of further education, the announcement of a Review of Vocational Qualifications in 1985 came as a welcome and long-awaited response to serious obstacles to greater participation and achievement in education and training. The experience of over a decade of projects, initiatives and programmes designed to mediate existing qualifications had left us convinced of the urgent need for government action to develop and control awards as either a prerequisite for or an accompaniment to the permanent reform of post-compulsory education and training.

Those recurrent experiments had also thrown up various practitioners' lists of characteristics necessary for any new qualifications system. Most of those lists included:

- rationalisation
- economy and cost-
    effectiveness
- accountability
- accessibility
- equity
- clarity and simplicity
- comprehensiveness
- valid and reliable assess-
    ment arrangements

- credit transfer
- standardisation
- transferability of
    learning
- flexible learning
    opportunities
- articulation between
    programmes
- progression opportunities
- multi-agency provision

These features were being sought for sound practical reasons to do with the patent unhelpfulness and unfairness of the range of qualifications on offer for so many of Further Education's clients.

Since the Review Group reported in 1986, progress towards the hoped-for system has been commendably swift. For vocational awards the language of assessment and certification is now being stabilised; awards are being presented in similar formats; supporting documentation for providers is developing a recognisable house-style; the case for breadth has been accepted; generic units common to different occupations are being drafted and a database is being designed. There are grounds for expecting clearer articulation between vocational and general education awards in the foreseeable future.

The emphasis on qualifications has a backwash effect on the internal organisation and culture of colleges. Structures and activities which do not readily align with the requirements of particular awards or awarding bodies, struggle to survive. Additional course components which are not connected to the prime qualification may be the first to go at times of constraint. Greater problems occur when integration is required across the awards of two or more bodies. Most colleges work with at least two distinct awarding bodies in each vocational area, and hesitate to press either body to move towards the other so as to support greater integration and economy. Until now it has usually seemed to college staff so much more sensible and realistic, given all the constraints, to keep on designing and offering distinct qualification courses, and to defer practical work on the frameworks and links required to optimise achievement and limit costs. As a result we are faced with a proliferation of courses and qualifications, and the lack of an overall framework for learning, assessment and certification. However, those external restrictions, which many FE colleges and personnel have become used to and internalised, are beginning to lift, and there is now a unique opportunity for FE to help create exciting new means of delivery for the new system of awards.

The first part of this chapter advocates a whole-college approach for the delivery of NVQs. In the second part I comment on the advocated approach by referring to the attempts of one college (Wirral Metropolitan College) to move in this direction.

THE RATIONALE FOR A NEW APPROACH

Despite the commitment and hard work which has gone into college and curriculum development during the last two decades, the results are mixed. There is much good practice, but this may still be vulnerable to marginal changes in funding and staff. As the Secretary of State for Education and Science has recently acknowledged, FE is still the least noticed part of the education system. It is also the most fragmented due to the sheer diversity of its students and provision, and to its many funding and controlling bodies. The plethora of smaller initiatives in FE over the last decade has demonstrated that things can be done differently for small numbers of people, and has rounded a few hard edges. However, these initiatives have not yet delivered their prime objectives: increased participation; a more informed and qualified public; greater personal, corporate, and public investment in, and support for, learners, education and training.

By and large it is still the case that syllabuses and lecturers constitute the conceptual centre and starting point for colleges; and that students are secondary. The student is still normally required to adjust him- or herself to an established curriculum and mode of delivery. Whatever the individual lecturer's or team's disposition, a College's organisation and structure tend to make this so. Too strong a focus on the teaching role can make the learning process a matter of covering the syllabus; narrow efficiency targets (such as a concentration of SSRs or minimum class sizes alone) can turn negotiation with students into covert persuasion or pressure.

Nevertheless, the various changes now underway for qualifications, and the context in which they are occurring, provides a window of opportunity for revitalising and developing FE on an exciting new basis. From having operated largely as a once-and-for-all service using a fairly restrictive array of qualifications, and offering limited progression opportunities, FE now has the possibility of becoming the essential intermediate component of an open education and training system based on unit credit transfer for individuals, and integrity for institutions.

Education and training is not value-free. A mature institution is one that is capable of working through and articulating its values and purposes. Given its greater autonomy and lack of shelter in the future, and the requirement to contribute to and win support within its locality, a college has to set out clearly what it stands for and is responsible for. A college has as a prime purpose the development of individuals and the certification of achievement. Therefore all of its values and purposes are bound to stem from and interact with the learner and his or her achievement.

For some years it has been widely agreed within FE that everything a college does can be regarded as the curriculum, because everything will have a bearing upon teaching and learning. Therefore institutional development should be 'curriculum-led' or 'curriculum-centred'. However, the curriculum has now got itself so tied up with courses, lecturers and teaching, and has become so elaborate and confused, that it has lost its sharpness of purpose, which is to serve the student and other clients. Everything a college does will have a bearing upon the personal development and achievement of the individual. Institutional development should therefore be 'achievement-led', testing all it does in a direct way against individual achievement, and regarding the curriculum as a resource rather than as a precious object in its own right.

Achievement-led institutional development is inherently reforming or corrective in nature. It therefore seeks to dispense with the industrial conservatism which may affect formal and informal relations within the college; with separate and different agreements and conduct for various groups of staff and students; with the teacher as the proxy and spokesperson for the learner; and with teaching as a proxy for learning. It recognises that an organization may be less mature than its members, and as a result may limit behaviour, to the detriment of human development and achievement.

A COLLEGE DELIVERY-STRUCTURE FOR NVQS

A large and complex organisation has to be managed strategically. By this I mean that its essential purpose has to be checked and made clear in the light of its current and future environment, and the fulfilment of its purpose needs to be measured and evaluated. Plans have also to be made at a range of levels and over a series of timescales; resources need to be acquired and priorities established; and monitoring should occur through a selection of indicators against agreed targets. These five steps are recurrent. Strategic management is cyclical, using cycles of various lengths. As far as possible it should be fresh and re-creative, building upon experience, but avoiding historical assumptions and conditioning.

A college which is being managed strategically will have identified the main implications of NCVQ in 1986 or 1987, and will have begun to take account of them at that stage. Colleges, however, cannot change overnight; nor can they shut down until they have taken on their new shape. Successful teaching and learning depends upon thousands of daily interactions which cannot be closely controlled. Therefore the process of radical change in a college requires considerable care, attention and safeguarding of services in order to prevent unwelcome knock-on effects for students, if for no other reason. The reasons for change have to be presented in a concrete, tangible way that enables staff to identify positive and practical routes forward and so feel confident that they can break out from traditional structures. Only then can they begin to develop such essentials as multi-disciplinary and inter-disciplinary courses, and broad-based courses with a common core and central thrust.

Other items that will need to be introduced are more student-activity-based learning, including actual work experience, and broad curriculum frameworks within which students can negotiate their own individual learning programmes. Consideration will have to be given to approaches to learning which suit the greater proportion of post-16 students staying in education and training, and to providing appropriate services for the greater number of adult students. College staff will have to turn their minds to non-traditional forms of access to knowledge; experiment with new and varied assessment techniques to include formative as well as summative aspects; and also try out new delivery systems such as open learning, distance learning, modular courses, etc.

Once all these aspects have been thought through, the next step is to seek a structure which can react to and accommodate change smoothly, minimise the effects of historical, environmental and social conditioning (ie individual attitudes), and present to students information regarding the full range of opportunities available in the context of the total curriculum, free from bias, prejudice and departmental self-interest. The quality of educational provision and student services must have priority over administrative expediency; and integration must be achieved alongside increased opportunities for staff to have personal centres of identity, linked with logical curriculum groupings. Such a structure should enhance the possibilities for self-actualisation and thereby achieve an improved organisational climate behind the scenes. These improvements need to be applied consistently across the college, encapsulating new initiatives as an integral part of its total work. In other words, the workload of the institution needs to be viewed as a total entity.

In addition the college should provide a back-up service to the curriculum, incorporating the building blocks which we know from experience, work in terms of student success (eg tutor groups and small units of achivement). Besides this there is always scope for improving communications, and thought should be given to maximising staff participation while at the same time minimising the bureaucracy of formal committee systems, etc.

At the present time many course teams and individual lecturers are simultaneously developing course statements, teaching materials, etc, which overlap and often duplicate each other. Such wasteful effort should be minimised. Efforts should also be made to achieve a balance and a partnership between teaching and support staff; to illustrate and clarify the authority system in the college and the points at which the resolution of issues should take place; to incorporate clear control mechanisms; and to identify the management levels in the organisation and delineate responsibilities at each level.

Staff and students need to be helped to have a clear understanding of the nature of the college, and staff need to see their priorities as:

- the highest possible standards in teaching and learning;
- the best possible guidance for students;
- the maintenance of up-to-date, relevant, and appropriate curricula.

Strategic management enables a college to respond to trends and events at an early stage, and as a result to give them the time they require for an adequate response. This is particularly important for major actions such as reorganisations, where the effects of misjudgements and error can be disastrous. By allocating generous time to reorganisation, one can underpin it with a series of supportive measures, and tie it in to concurrent activity, such as the planning and implementation of the TVEI Extension, and Work Related Further Education planning cycles. A generous time-scale also improves the quality of thinking within the organisation, and can make a reality of consultation by incorporating fresh ideas from all sources.

A COLLEGE MISSION

A basic requirement of an organisation is that it has a purpose. FE colleges have since their inception suffered from a lack of agreed role and purpose. Restructuring, or reviewing, has to be seized as an opportunity to clarify the colleges' values and purposes, and to set these out in a mission statement. The process of establishing the mission is valuable in bringing into the open essential issues which FE must debate and resolve if students are to move freely around colleges and the service, within a comprehensive qualifications system. The debate has to have integrity, and to be rooted in practice; it should not simply be rhetorical. Devices such as mission statements must be true to the broad intentions and movement of the individual college; otherwise they should not be used. Writing a mission statement is the easy part; embedding it and making the vision a practical reality is a harder and endless challenge. Wirral Metropolitan College's efforts at embedding its mission statement are set out on page 46.

A CURRICULUM FRAMEWORK

A mission statement puts the learner and his or her achievement at the centre of things, demands that the college organise around personal achievement rather than curriculum and courses. The curriculum becomes only as important as the ends it serves. There is an enormous amount of literature on the FE curriculum, together with widely endorsed principles of access, progression, autonomy, relevance, breadth, differentiation and coherence. However their meanings have largely been defined within narrow parameters by educationalists for educationalists, and their existence is much more evident to lecturers, teachers and educational managers than to learners. We have to recognise the abstraction, paternalism and vulnerability to feedback and inspection of much of our curriculum development, given that we cannot yet articulate pre-16 provision with post-16, nor general education with vocational, and that increasingly in FE young people and mature adults learn together and require a common approach.

For achievement-led institutional development the curriculum has to be redefined in terms which can be directly recognised and accepted by the learner, and engaged in directly by him or her with specialist information and advice, but without a lot of mediation or interpretation. Ideally the learner should be as self-directed within a college as he or she would expect to be elsewhere, and be entitled to receive a range of learning, assessment and certification services according to his or her needs, aspirations and circumstances. When taken forward into actual services, this approach significantly expands and diversifies the college offering, and breaks down the clear distinctions between lecturers' roles and support staff's roles. The new array of services becomes the collective responsibility of the whole college in a direct, integrated and thoroughly practical sense.

This means, for example, that coherence is a matter for the learner to determine, and not the lecturer or institution. Coherence emerges through the relationship formed between the learner and the various services provided for him or her, rather than in the mind of the provider. Coherence can occur when the college responds to individual need and circumstances within a progressive system of credits. Coherence is not necessarily the same thing as continuity.

Therefore a new set of learning principles emerges, the headings for which might be:

- recurrence
- advocacy
- flexibility
- empowerment
- personal acheivement
- visibility
- learning support

Once defined further, these can give rise to a series of objectives. For example, 'personal achievement' can be defined as follows:

1 The motivating effect of personal achievement should be optimised.
2 Programmes should recognise and build upon learners' prior achievements.
3 Under-prepared learners should have the means of acquiring the essential preliminary achievements for entry to courses and programmes without delay, and where possible as part of course entry.
4 Assessment and reviews of progress should be incorporated in all learners' programmes.
5 The learner should have in his or her keeping an action plan showing, among other things, achievement targets and achievements gained.
6 Assessment should at all times be visible to and understood by the learner.
7 Supplementary and reinforcement learning should be available to assist learners.
8 Learners should be able to test their progress and achievements on demand.

These objectives, and those derived from the other headings, can provide a basis for the overall learning framework, and the individual learning opportunity within that framework. For Wirral Metropolitan College's action planning which derived from this analysis, see page 50.

PRACTICAL ASPECTS OF DELIVERY

So far, this chapter has described a means for FE of reviewing its fitness to deliver personal achievement and qualifications within a progressive system of credits. By developing and embracing the concepts of achievement-led institutional development colleges gain the means of identifying, sifting, evaluating and responding to the various national and international developments associated with assessment and certification. By standing behind the student rather than any of his or her proxies the college is able to regard courses and classes as one delivery option among many, and to avoid a psychological dependency upon current ways of doing things. However, this does not mean that change is straightforward; most of the parts needed for the new approach will have yet to be assembled and organised into a full delivery system for comprehensive unit credit transfer. Nevertheless, the vision which a college may now have of comprehensive arrangements to generate and optimise personal achievement will enable it to revitalise its talent and resources and step out of its old skin.

It may be helpful now to think of the 'old' and the 'new' or alternative college, the old college having done a good job in past circumstances, but needing now to re-create itself in an exciting new form. Each change has to help the old to become the new by supporting the mission in a practical sense. No college can afford to delay practical measures until the values and principles underlying them have been thoroughly worked through and subscribed to. An interactive and reciprocal process is needed, which involves rapid practical activity alongside and integrated with the refinement of ideas and communication. So the vision must be continuously informed, tested and taken forward by practice.

A collegiate admissions procedure

Traditionally access to much of FE has been through an enrolment process which has been heavily influenced by institutional priorities. Enrolment has often been a short-term effort carried out in a frenzy of activity during the first two or three days of the Autumn term. After this the tables and posters have been removed; the rooms have been hastily converted back to classrooms, and all vestiges of the process have disappeared. Late enquiries and enrolments have then been dealt with by administrative staff who have usually not been trained to give educational information and advice. Young full-time students may have had more sustained attention if they applied several months before September. However, the ease and quality of their access may also have been variable.

One consequence of this approach has been that colleges as a whole have not had a clear picture of the total volume of enquiries, or of the number of potential learners who have not come into the college for one reason or another.

In recent years colleges have found various ways of modifying and enhancing their enrolment procedures. This is fortunate, since the traditional approach is no longer appropriate for the new qualifications and learning frameworks which are based on individualised, differentiated programmes.

Assessment and the accreditation of prior achievement

Any attempt to improve the process of entry to a college involves assessment. Initial diagnostic assessment, together with the accreditation of prior acheivement, is essential to prevent recruitment and course entry from being arbitrary and inefficient. To bring this about requires:

1 a set of standards against which to assess potential students;
2 a means of accepting or acquiring, and validating, evidence of achievement;
3 capable and trained staff, other resources and structures which fulfil the assessment activity.

The standards are needed to give a means of identifying entry and progression through work-based and educational routes. They must be reliable and acceptable, not arbitrary. At present the major sources of standards for colleges are from Lead Industry Bodies, NCVQ and from the National Curriculum.

The immediate next step is to design a format on which to record the standard in a consistent way, give instructions for acquiring evidence of achievement against the given standard, give guidance on available assessment materials and refer to the standard's currency. The formats adopted by Scotvec, CPVE (preparatory modules) and Mainframe units are helpful sources for this.

The effect of all this emphasis on standards and the establishing of achievement will obviously be an explosion of demand for assessment, and for flexible course frameworks to be accessed as needed rather than taken as a whole. The college response at this early stage may need to be twofold: first to expand its individual study and assessment facilities to include flexible learning workshops, an assessment centre, a study centre with help facilities, a careers centre, and an exit and transfer service, and second to start the large-scale and long-term task of converting courses to learning frameworks.

Modularisation and common learning outcomes

The previously described changes put courses under considerable pressure, as do the changes in demography now facing FE. A review of college courses as a whole in the light of a new focus on personal achievement will highlight the need to:

1 adapt set courses to accommodate students' varied attainments and needs at entry (ie, flexible modularised courses);
2 adjust provision to the students' personal attainment targets (ie, offer a choice of modules to individual students according to their agreed action plans);
3 communicate their outcomes to enable personal records to be maintained;

4 make informed decisions about the organisation of courses in relation to action plans and units of credit.

The use of NCVQ's National Record of Vocational Achievement within colleges brings to the foreground these issues. By linking together personal achievements to a national system, the National Record highlights the need for individual action plans, and a system of assessment that supports the learning process. The National Record also links achievement to a national system of credit accumulation, to facilitate greater access to qualifications.

CONCLUSION

FE colleges are as varied as their origins, history and environment might lead one to expect. They have learned to make a virtue out of necessity by being responsive and opportunist within ad hoc and localised post-compulsory education and training arrangements. However, although colleges can be stimulating and adventurous places to work and learn in because they are so protean, it is time for them to be better thought out, more visible and understandable to the population as a whole, and more adept at supporting, assessing, and enhancing personal development and achievement.

Since certification gets to the heart of all FE colleges, NVQs have to be seen as much more than the signal for a new set of qualifications which can be dealt with as they arise, one by one. It is in keeping with the ideals of FE to acknowledge the power of assessment as a learning tool; to appreciate the effectiveness of modular programme design as a means of stretching achievement in all directions; and to exploit NCVQ's long-term goals in order significantly to increase participation and achievement in education and training. Whatever the health of a college, a holistic response to NCVQ is called for in order to optimise the remarkable opportunity which it represents to establish FE as the essential intermediate component of a progressive education and training system.

WIRRAL METROPOLITAN COLLEGE'S RESPONSE IN ACTION

Wirral Metropolitan College, a group 10 college set in the Wirral between the Rivers Mersey and Dee, has over 6,000 students aged 16 to 18 (half full-time and half part-time), and over 17,000 adult students on various qualifications. Entry to the courses is not normally restricted by age, and most of the students learn in all-age groups. I shall now describe the college's early attempts to capitalise on the new freedoms and opportunities presented by NCVQ.

The College's response so far to NCVQ is holistic in two respects. It is approaching NCVQ as an important feature of an external environment which contains many other related and different issues which must be addressed simultaneously. It also recognises that since qualifications have been a major, and often the main, determinant of FE colleges' thinking and actions so far, a radical change in qualifications requires an equivalent conceptual and behavioural change within the College itself. As a strategy, achievement-led institutional development embodies most of what Wirral Met is thinking about and moving towards.

In November 1986 an inspection of Wirral Met by a team of HMIs highlighted among many good features a number of limitations. These were examined in the light of emerging trends and require-ments, and a list of issues was drawn up for attention through a major College Review. Among other observations made by the HMI team, they concluded that there were deficiencies in the College's informa-tion and counselling for students regarding the full range of opportunities available, and that the College's perceptions about various categories of students were unsatisfactory. They noted that it was difficult to achieve sustained inter-departmental co-operation. This was particularly noticeable in relation to the operation and development of courses which needed the co-operation and support of two or more departments; the sharing of resources; the co-ordination of staff from different departments; and making staff available to share and participate in curriculum development. Further, they thought that there was inadequate understanding and contact between the academic and vocational aspects of College provision, that the College lacked a corporate image to the communities it serves, and that there was a degree of organisational confusion resulting from the strategies adopted to cope with an inflexible formal structure. The HMIs also detected a serious lack of various support services to the main teaching activity, and a sense of frustration among many staff at the lack of opportunity for them to gain recognition and to contribute to aspects of curriculum and institutional development. Finally, they saw an increasing need for a new type of co-ordination function to ensure the proper contribution, co-operation and control of all functions and agencies across the College.

So it was clear to the College in 1987 that it lacked the elements and characteristics required to deliver a new qualifications system, or, indeed, to cope positively with other emerging trends and require-ments. Therefore the College embarked on a major Review, giving itself nine months to arrive at an action plan, and a further 12 months to complete its implementation. A form of discrepancy analysis was used, with consultation occurring at the five stages of position statementing, environmental scanning, objective setting, strategic planning and action planning.

Wirral Met is a large college based on three main sites, with over 500 full-time staff and as many part-timers. It had been through several reorganisations before 1987, and many staff perceived change negatively. So the reasons for change had to be presented in a very concrete way, in order to get agreement that the College had to catch up with changes in students, learning and assessment noted earlier in this chapter.

The final choice of structure comprised five large faculties embracing virtually all the College's courses and programmes; with a number of sections and lateral functions within each faculty. In addition, a College Services Faculty was designed to encourage and sustain whole-college approaches and an ever-increasing student orientation.

THE WIRRAL COLLEGE MISSION

A fundamental issue for Wirral Met in 1987 was its lack of agreed or tangible identity. This was again an issue which needed to be resolved through the reviewing process, and not imposed or tacked on. A commitment to develop a clear mission was given at the outset of the Review, and thus was set at the head of a list of the elements needed to encourage continuous change in a spirit of confidence and optimism. The list of elements included:

- a clear mission for the College;
- objectives for developing staff to fulfil the mission;
- measures to reinforce staff commitment to the agreed way forward;
- the capacity to develop staff;
- practical action programmes linked to and inclusive of all staff;
- adequate resources;
- regular reviews of progress.

However, it took a further nine months of observation, thought, and discussion in a range of settings to develop the rationale of achievement-led institutional development from which our College Mission Statement derived. The core of the College mission is personal achievement. The Mission Statement notes:

1 Personal achievement is every individual's right, and the College should organise itself behind this right.
2 The establishment of personal achievement is a powerful aid to learning and motivation; it should be seen primarily in these terms, within a framework of standards.
3 The physical, mental and psychological involvement of learners with their own development and achievement, and that of their peers, should be adopted as an organising principle for the College.
4 Personal achievement should constitute the core mission of the College. To encourage the College to be self-critical about its ability and preparedness to support personal growth, positive appraisal measures should be introduced and developed for learning, teaching and learner support.

This core section of the mission is the College's equivalent of NCVQ's basic statement of its purpose which appears in most of its publications. Being concerned with the local delivery of learning and credit, the College Mission Statement can emphasise the beneficial effects for personal growth of a clear entitlement to achieve and to have that achievement recognised. The statement is not simply aspirational though: it fixes personal achievement as an organisational principle, to be incorporated in the College's structure and operations.

In its three main sections, the College Mission Statement addresses:

- the need to define a mission for the College;
- the mission itself;
- fulfilling the mission.

Woven into it are five associated and supportive themes:

- learner involvement and empowerment
- institutional appraisal and self scrutiny
- needs analysis and responsiveness
- human resource development
- reflective management.

These come together to represent an organisation with consistent principles and approaches throughout.

Having personal achievement at the core of the College mission does not imply any diminution in standards or any disregard for corporate clients. A focus on personal achievement actually concentrates attention on standards and their purposes. The commitment to working directly with the learner, and to following his or her lead, helps those standards to be internalised and embedded. The College mission finds no contradication between its commitment to the individual and its responsibilities to company and economic development. Under the section 'Relatedness to Industry' the Mission Statement reads as follows.

1 The College should aim for a precise relationship with local business and industry in order to contribute to the locality's economic well-being and development.

2 This relationship should be active and predictive, and involve joint planning so that human resources can be developed in tandem with organisational, infra-structural and economic development.

3 More broadly, the College should develop its services to reflect a future marked by increased skill and intellectual requirements, individual mobility, the growth of international factors, and changed management-labour relations.

To have value, a mission has to become part of College life. Since the draft mission statement was consulted upon and endorsed in late 1988, it has been printed to a very high quality and circulated to all College staff and associates; built into the staff development programme and into recruitment and appointment procedures; incorporated into work-related further education and TVEI Extension proposals and planning; and used as a touchstone for planning.

The most interesting use of the Statement so far has been among the College's middle management team. In June 1988, 25 staff likely to be middle managers in the new structure embarked on a training programme. At the outset members of the group demonstrated a number of characteristics and perceptions which needed to change radically if the College was to move forward as required. There were personal and idiosyncratic notions of FE based on individual past experience only: thus, FE might be seen as for 16–19-year-olds only. Values were at times confused or covert, and were frequently linked to self-interest: hence, advanced work was justified as being 'better' than non-advanced. Inappropriate industrial practices were being called on to carry out or justify managerial roles and actions; seniority was often equated with power and the possession of information. Colleagues' capability and contributions tended to be recognised or denied on the basis of their Burnham grades. Internal competition and suspicion were accepted, widespread and often automatic.

For six months the team focused on the College Mission Statement by basing projects on it. The projects were:

1 to interrogate the Statement, through an analysis of staff's reactions to it;
2 marketing;
3 human resource development in FE;
4 staff recruitment and selection;
5 the skills of middle management in FE.

As a result of this activity it is evident that the team have begun to shift their allegiance from department to college, and from college to service. They have learned to articulate and debate their values, and to cluster around an agreed value system. This has led to evaluation criteria and techniques being developed for middle managers. The team's thinking has moved from courses, lecturers and teaching, to learners, learning and assessment. A common language has developed, incorporating certain key words as mental building blocks: achievement, assessment, framework, entitlement.

From the middle management group we know that 85 per cent of the College staff have read the Mission Statement, and that 58 per cent believe that it should be afforded high priority. Interestingly, we know from the group that the sections of the mission regarding access, entitlement and progression are subject to most debate among staff as a whole. It is all too easy to assume that staff are in accord about these principles, when large elements of FE provision are actually alien to them in their origins.

Within Wirral Met, the understanding gained on all sides by the actual process of restructuring is quite evident. This is not to say that there are not major disagreements over direction and priorities: quite the reverse, and the College is the healthier for them. It is recognised that the new structure constitutes an act of faith in the College's human resources, who have practised the approaches needed through the process of restructuring; that it incorporates opportunities and incentives for change and development; that it can flex in order to cope with and optimise change; and that it enables control with a lightness of touch.

A comprehensive review of Wirral Met was called for because the College's internal organisation and activity reflected the lack of coherence in post-compulsory education, training and certification generally. I have described how over two years both purpose and structure for the College have been worked through using the achievement of the individual as the main vision and organisational principle. This has, we hope, led to a structure which, with constant fine-tuning, will be able to bear an ever-increasing range of learning, assessment and certification services, and a growing band of staff with new work roles.

THE WIRRAL'S CURRICULUM FRAMEWORK

Wirral Met is in the first wave of TVEI Extension programmes post-16. In planning for this our course analyses convinced us that quality and development required a fresh approach which was not reflected in the initial TVEI guidance, but which accorded with NCVQ's long-term goals to get rid of restrictions on age, attendance patterns and time bases, and to facilitate credit accumulation. The College therefore worked through the alternative curriculum principles referred to in the first part of this chapter, and eventually produced a five-year action plan as the basis of its TVEI Extension programme.

These are the main headings of the Five-Year Action Plan.

1 To create a College which is strikingly ahead of its current image and activity.
2 To plan and develop a collegiate admissions service.
3 To plan and introduce a range of student support services including counselling, study centres, careers centres and work placement units.
4 To plan, introduce and evaluate a universally available core curriculum framework which includes continuing learning and achievement in communication, mathematics, information technology and science.
5 To plan and introduce individual learning programmes for all major vocational routes, based upon learning centres.
6 To plan, introduce and evaluate assessment on demand for the core, individual and open learning programmes, and for a selection of vocational competencies.
7 To design and introduce a summative assessment and certification service which links with the range of current qualifications on offer, and those which will emerge through NCVQ and SEAC.
8 To plan and introduce an exit and transfer service.
9 To develop the College's marketing practices to include family and weekend learning, summer schools, and assessment and placement services for employers.
10 To exchange and disseminate information and experience for the benefit of the College, its users and clients, and the service generally.

All ten objectives are being addressed from the outset; clearly, though, whereas some, like the collegiate admissions service, can be put in place fairly quickly, others will take the full five years, and will partly depend on external bodies fulfilling their own objectives. Paramount among these is NCVQ, which is presently sponsoring a College NCVQ Development Officer to monitor and comment on the College's progress towards the viable delivery of transferable units of credit on a large scale. The Training Agency has also strongly endorsed and supported the approach in so far as our TVEI Extension programme is concerned.

DELIVERY

During 1989 the College introduced elements of a delivery service for units of credit in three phases: student admissions and records; initial assessment and the accreditation of prior achievement; and modularisation and generic units. Each of these is addressed in more detail below, with the greatest attention being devoted to the first stage, since that has now been completed and documented.

A collegiate admissions procedure

For Wirral Met the task of transforming our admissions practices has represented a major task in infra-structural change. The year 1987 was not a good one for our potential students, since industrial action largely halted the customary informal arrangements for giving information and advice during July and August. That, together with the clear limitations of the departmentalised admissions procedures for full-time students, made the reform of our admissions procedures an urgent priority. Therefore in May 1988 a basic admissions service started as a supplement to the traditional one, and comprised:

1 small admissions offices placed prominently in the three main college foyers;
2 the appointment of a team of student admissions officers (SAOs);
3 measures to ensure a constant supply of good quality materials;
4 a referrals procedure to lecturers, the careers service, adult guidance service, employment training and YTS programmes.

Between June and October 1988 the SAOs dealt with 2,600 enquiries. Nearly half of these were by telephone; others resulted from a variety of publicity events, open days, personal calls, letters and other contacts. These figures and other positive feedback endorsed the need for the type of mediation between the public's enquiries and our

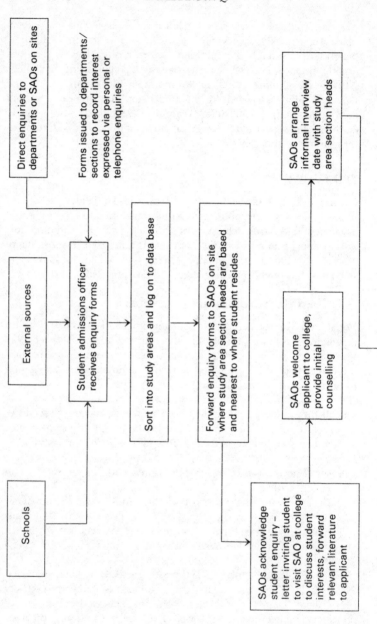

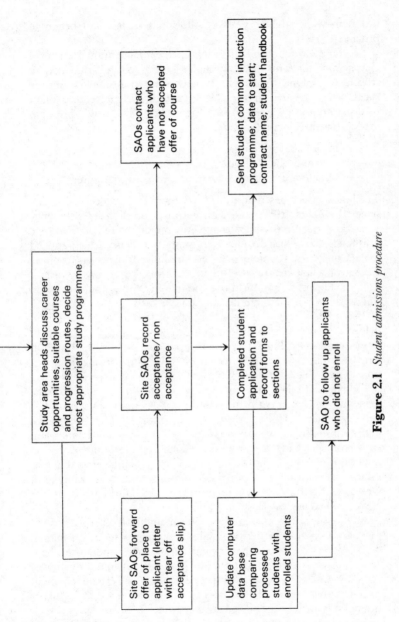

Figure 2.1 *Student admissions procedure*

provision which this very basic admissions service had begun to provide.

By May 1988 an informal development team had drafted a series of charts and diagrams which visualised the College's direction in various ways. One of these charts demonstrated in simple terms the types of services which a collegiate admissions procedure might incorporate and give rise to (see Figure 2.1). The new admissions process has three main functions:

- informing and advising;
- admission to the College;
- enrolment and induction on to a course or programme.

The fuller service based on these three functions has been operating since December 1988, and concentrated on full-time students' admissions during the pilot year. This piloting complemented the introduction of TVEI Extension for post-16 students, which applied to the College from September 1989. This fuller admissions procedure is based on a flow-diagram (see Figure 2.1) covering actions by various staff, the lines of communication, and the time limits applied to each stage. All supporting materials are standardised.

The main elements of the admissions procedure are as described below. A team of six admissions officers gives around 120 hours of service each week. This is increased for peak periods of public interest. The team has clear job descriptions, training, support and feedback procedures. The admissions service falls within the Learner Services Section of the College Services Faculty. The section is founded on the principles of student entitlement and advocacy, and its success in the new structure is to be judged on that basis. In this section the admissions officers work alongside the careers co-ordinator and careers officers, and the college counsellors. The admissions officers do not simply operate on the College sites. They respond to invitations for information and advice within the community, and increasingly work with school staff to set up simple transfer procedures and align the school and college offering.

An interview with an admissions officer enables a potential student to work through his or her personal plans, aspirations and problems. The officer seeks and logs personal details, offers guidance about routes of progression, and normally arranges an initial diagnostic assessment, plus meetings with specialist tutors. Where the potential student appears to need other specialist help before exploring his or her options further, the officer arranges this.

A computerised 'expert' system is being developed to support the officers and to encourage learner involvement in selecting courses and programmes. The computer programme, which is currently being evaluated, enables learners to input information concerning their age, qualifications, previous experience, preferred mode of attendance, vocational interests, etc, in order to obtain guidance on courses and programmes to meet their needs.

New enquiry and application forms have been designed to complement the collegiate approach to admissions, and establish a basis for an individual student records system. A database has been set up to provide detailed information for the College and faculties on enquiries and responses. This database is at present separate from the main college management information system, but will in time be incorporated within it. Even in its present basic form the information is providing valuable feedback on which to base the next development phase of our admissions procedures.

Given the potential benefits of modularised programmes the College can now seriously address the question of over- and under-prepared learners. Therefore in the core areas of communication, mathematics, information technology, and science, computer-aided diagnostic assessments are being developed. These subjects are essential building blocks for entry into further and higher education. Pilot assessments have been carried out, and our initial evaluation indicates great enthusiasm by learners and staff for this approach, which offers immediate feedback. Equally important, the technology and software now available and being used give us the means of providing assessment on demand either as part of a learning programme, or as an independent service. It will be essential to maintain the integrity of computer-based assessment, and procedures are being designed for the training and licensing of lecturers in the design and use of these assessment techniques.

The way in which students are informed, guided and admitted to a college prepares them for their role as students thereafter. It is of little use being interactive and participative within courses if the means of entry have been one-sided and crude. Therefore a skilled and objective admissions process is an essential early step in developing an infrastructure for delivering NVQs.

Modularisation and common learning outcomes

The steps taken so far have included designing an overall curriculum framework which incorporates all the components subscribed to by the College and required by our various funding bodies. The framework has been published internally in a series of bulletins. Next, the courses being offered within each faculty are being aggregated into larger entities with certain key components, such as a common core with flexible delivery and a range of explicit standards or learning outcomes, with the means of attaining their outcomes organised into units or modules; with firm arrangements for formative assessment and reviewing; and with records of achievement tied into the NROVA.

The intention is to turn separate courses into an overall framework within a three-to-five-year timescale by a series of aggregations against a common curriculum framework. This timescale is dictated by the time it takes to revalidate provision, to check our progress and make adjustments as we go along, and for the work being undertaken by the various national bodies (NCC, SEAC, NCVQ and LIBs especially) to come to fruition.

The first large suite of courses for adjustment are the BTEC First and National Diplomas in Mechanical Engineering, Electrical and Electronic Engineering, Construction and Science under the broad heading of Awards in Technology. We have attempted to incorporate in the new framework the opportunities which each previous course has offered to its own students, but which have not extended across all the courses. The discussions leading to the new programme have been fascinating. They have illustrated the confusion which can exist within course teams between processes and outcomes, and over what a college can and can not do within its course approvals. They have demonstrated the need for substantial staff training and support in delivery methods, and in the operational meaning of competence and its constituent parts. They have highlighted the complexity of the relationship between learning, time, and credit value in unit-based courses. The discussions have also strikingly reinforced the feedback from the Mission Statement regarding individual entitlement, in demonstrating the way in which highly committed college staff may regard themselves as serving a vocational sector, a particular trade, or even an examining and validating body, in a narrow way, and may sometimes let this loyalty obscure the rights of individuals. Most of all, though, they have generated energy and creativity at the level of the tutorial team where, in a purposeful institution with a live mission, quality has to be engendered and sustained.[1]

NOTE

1 This chapter is based on a series of working documents which are available from the Wirral Metropolitan College for the cost of printing and postage.

3. The college marketing implications of NVQs

Ernest Theodossin

Effective marketing is about responding to customer needs instead of trying to clear the shelves of unwanted goods. As the PICKUP definition[1] puts it, 'marketing is the creative process of satisfying customer needs profitably'.

The process is *creative* because it takes considerable imagination to step figuratively outside one's own skin and into that of another person, to view one's products through the purchaser's eyes. Whoever is responsible for marketing the college has to make a conscious and continual effort to keep the customer viewpoint firmly within the institution's gaze.

How, then, do National Vocational Qualifications (NVQs) look from a customer perspective? Which needs can we expect them to satisfy and which might they leave unmet? What problems might NVQ marketing encounter? To what extent are NVQs likely to represent a better customer deal?

THREATS AND OPPORTUNITIES

Student and employer markets – further education's (FE) traditional customer groups – have been changing dramatically for some time, a situation which can be regarded as either disturbing or encouraging for colleges.

On the negative side, there are declining sales figures. Few teachers can still be unaware that whereas in the past most college business relied on school leavers, recruiting from this segment has become progressively difficult. The demographic downturn of young people has led to competition for the post-compulsory market from employers, private trainers, schools, other FE and (in the course of the 1990s) higher education colleges. One result is that full-time students have become rarer in many colleges. In addition, the demise of appreticeships has reduced the volume of college day-release activity, and the proliferation of small businesses has increased the number of employers who cannot afford to train staff during business hours because one pair of absent hands can create major operational problems. At the same time Training Agency youth programmes have stressed on-the-job experience at the expense of the off-the-job kind and have frequently favoured contributions from private sector trainers.

The popular notion that falling rolls can be counteracted by better advertising, glossier prospectuses and more aggressive selling does not always survive close examination. What was once a seller's market for FE has become a buyer's market, which does not mean that colleges should abandon efforts to maintain their share of traditional markets, but that survival in anything like their present size and number requires colleges to penetrate new markets.

All is not doom and gloom, however. Marketing opportunities abound for most UK colleges. On the positive side, we should note both government pressure to increase the level of workforce training in advance of the single market in 1992 and the very real need for such training: 'Only 40 per cent of the UK workforce hold relevant qualifications, a considerably lower proportion than in other industrial countries with which we compete.'[2] We are not a comparatively well-educated or well-trained country. Outside the 16–19 segment, the market is anything but saturated.

The main opportunities lie in marketing to adults and employers – in training, reskilling and updating. This market, however, will not often fit comfortably into existing college arrangements, which have evolved over the decades to accommodate the very distinctive kinds of customers who are now in short supply.

Major changes are required if colleges are to meet the new challenge. For example, those who design and/or provide training programmes need to think not solely in terms of adolescents but also of people in their twenties, thirties, forties – and up, since the effects of the reduced birthrate in the 1970s are expected to lead to an extended working life for many people (in other countries up to age 70). College amenities and facilities have often been designed to lure those school leavers for whom somewhere to smoke, play pop music, pursue sporting interests and socialise is a key consideration. The expectations of the adult workforce are often quite different. So, too, are their requirements for physical comfort and cleanliness, canteen and library provision. It should also be noted that inherited resourcing formulas make full-time FE students (mostly 16–19) much more valuable than part-time adults: it can take up to 20 (or more) part-timers to equal what is represented by selling one place on a two-year full-time course – something like the difference between trying to make a living by selling roller skates rather than cars.

Nor is it only increased selling effort which is required to fill part-time courses: their construction and delivery are also more demanding. In the background, as they strive still harder to recruit their traditional 16–19 full-timers, college staff are aware of the dilemmas. For example, a growing number (often the majority) of college students are women, a market-place change which needs to be reflected in course provision and delivery, as well as (in many colleges) appropriate créche facilities. In some areas an increasing proportion of college students are (or ought to be) drawn from ethnic minorities and the disabled – people whose special needs have course delivery implications. Also adult workers are limited in their availability for training, not only because of the location of their workplaces, but also because of private responsibilities and commitments.

As we move into the 1990s, sales opportunities abound, but different markets require diffrent approaches and make different demands. Without major changes in organisation, resourcing, and reward systems, penetrating new markets will remain a difficult task.

THE MARKETING ATTRACTIONS OF NVQs

The National Council for Vocational Qualifications (NCVQ) can be seen as helping in numerous ways to meet the needs of the new markets. A comprehensive recognition of what is required is inherent in its list of 15 framework objectives.[3] Those which are perhaps most central to effective marketing are as follows.

1 The activities of 'about 300 bodies' – a notoriously imprecise figure – awarding qualifications in England, Northern Ireland and Wales are being brought into simplified and systematised order. Sorting out what was a widely acknowledged muddle can only help with the marketing of training.
2 College marketing units ought to find it easier to sell products whose market-place value is clarified through the use of such devices as the NVQ 'kitemark', designated competency levels, and links with and equivalency among the various awards (including those in Scotland).
3 NCVQ strongly supports the use of 'modular modes of delivery'. These can assist (but have not always done so) with the development of a credit system, a useful form of customer

banking which can facilitate self-paced learning, the recording of achievement, career path divergence, etc.

4 NVQs are 'based on employment led standards of competence' and are aimed at a fuller involvement of employers, which ought to ensure training which is relevant to the workplace.

5 There is a commitment to recognising 'prior achievement' which, by definition, large numbers of adults must possess.

6 Vocational qualifications are to be delivered flexibly by being 'appropriately independent of the mode, duration and location of learning'.

7 'Particular needs' are to be 'taken fully into account in the provision made'.

8 Developments are to be encouraged to promote vocational education and training which provide 'quick reaction to changes in technology, markets and occupations'.

All of this is impressive and encouraging to anyone involved in marketing education and training. The emphasis is on bringing order from chaos, recognising individual needs (credit accumulation, advanced standing, varied delivery) and market-place value (job relevance, speed).

It would, however, be a mistake to assume that a training system can be made customer-centred solely through activity at national level, or that the promulgation by committees of unchallengeable sentiments will automatically result in dramatic changes in this classroom or that workshop. In FE, delivery is very much a local business, run by particular teachers working with individual students.

If the new awards are to meet the training needs of 20,000,000 people in the workforce as well as of adolescents and the unwaged, the marketing implications of the new system at college level need to be explored and taken on board by college managers.

MARKETING NVQ TO THE COLLEGE

A new training award system makes enormous demands on all college staff. It is therefore necessary to train people to understand the new qualifications and to encourage them to support the new objectives. No manufacturing firm, for example, would introduce an entirely new product range without simultaneously investing in staff training. Those involved in selling need to know their products. From a marketing perspective, it is important to accept the following:

1 Both teachers and support staff will work (or not) the new system and both need training, not least front-of-house staff (telepho-

nists, receptionists) who are the first point of contact for most new customers, and who are likely to have to field awkward and complex questions.

2 The training ought to include not only giving information but also opportunities for staff to explore the implications, and time to understand the benefits and how to present them to customers.

3 Training staff to operate a new system cannot be a one-off activity (eg two days in September), but needs to occur over time as problems surface and implications reveal themselves.

If NVQ is to be effectively presented to the market-place, the new system must itself be marketed to college staff.

BROADCASTING THE MESSAGE

Colleges have a promotional role with NVQs. However much is done in this area by NCVQ, colleges will for some time need to support NVQs locally by conducting information campaigns aimed at schools and school leavers, parents and employers. The market needs to be educated to understand NVQs, how they differ from what was on offer previously, how they improve on it and what benefits they provide. In turn, that has promotional implications for colleges.

1 The same communication modes will not suit everyone. Colleges need to distribute printed material (leaflets, booklets, charts, posters), make videos available, give talks to public groups and run information stalls (in the college, shopping centres, super-markets, etc).

2 The same messages will not be appropriate for all groups. The Scottish Action Plan, for example, was presented to the public with different booklets for employers, parents and students – each of which group has distinctive concerns and individual needs. And within a generic group, such as students, one needs to be wary of the varying concerns of young initial trainees and of adults involved in mid-career reskilling or updating.

3 The same presentational style cannot be effective with different groups. Language, tone, and visual components such as colour and artwork need to be varied for different groups.

4 If you wish to communicate effectively, you need to use the recipients' vocabularly. Technical terms and jargon which have not yet been acquired are inappropriate. So, too, are acronyms and sets of initials, the kind of coded language which means something only to club members.

The conventional argument for not changing award systems (the public will be confused) may well prove once again accurate if appropriate resources are not directed towards promoting the new system in the college market-place.

ACKNOWLEDGING ACHIEVEMENTS

Few teachers appreciate how important a part *time* plays in education and training. For generations, learning has been parcelled out in timetables (hours, weeks, terms, years) and there has been an implicit assumption that for the same qualification (a certificate, diploma or degree) the same time is required for all subjects and for all students – even through at a practical level teachers recognise that people learn at different rates.

Education and training have also traditionally been activities of the young, for which reason courses and programmes have often been long enough to allow learners to grow up. In dealing with the adult population, this is no longer a requirement: time serving needs to give way to the notion of competency.

Assessment of prior learning and achivement (APLA) is bound to be seen as disturbing by some lecturers because it reduces the boundaries between workplace and college and, where staff are involved in its certification, it involves teachers in making predictive judgements. It also raises a number of technical and management problems which need to be dealt with at local level. These include such questions as:

- Who is to be responsible for the assessing?
- Where is it to be done?
- How is it to be done?
- Who will pay for it?
- Will dissatisfied applicants have rights of appeal?
- How will the consequences of positive assessment be monitored?

The last question refers to results in both the workplace and the college. Not all adults will necessarily want APLA in order to gain advanced standing on a course. Some will wish to use their paper certification as a work passport. In either case, assessment will need to be shown to be valid if the market-place value of both the certification and any subsequent qualification towards which it is used are not to suffer.

We are still, unfortunately, at the stage of confronting APLA issues. Even though work is in hand, much more remains to be done. We ought also to remind ourselves how slowly education moves: modular courses, credit transfer, open learning, self-paced learning, etc. – most of these have been bandied about by educationalists for decades, but in their British manifestations are still in embryonic form compared to the best overseas arrangements.

CUSTOMISED SHORT COURSES

There are strong indications that customised short courses rather than the formal award-bearing variety will meet many of the demands for a better trained workforce in the 1990s. As a result, bespoke provision for industry is a college growth area. Many forces (particularly of the market variety) have produced this situation.

Despite Government commitment (noted above) to promoting a more 'qualified' workforce, employers are understandably preoccupied with cost effectiveness and with speed in overcoming skill shortages. Such concerns have consequently stimulated the demand for customised offerings.

The Training Agency has developed its own short courses and funded others, often through the promotion of training needs analysis (TNA). Private trainers have responded to what is potentially a lucrative market. Employers can commission training from the Open College. Many local authority colleges have set up short-course units and private college companies to mop up demand.

Whoever produces it and however it emerges, by definition, customised training cannot often be identical to the 'units' of standard courses. Nor can it be ignored as a form of training: the result is an interesting marketing challenge for both colleges and NCVQ.

From an employee perspective all provision (wherever and by whomever delivered) is a part of the individual's training profile and ought to be treated as such. Equally, if TNA is to give to both employers and employees the kind of support they require, its recommendations will have to be linked to award-bearing courses, and colleges will need to develop appropriate databases to ensure that customer achievements have been recorded. In the United States, short customised courses run for employers are often 'credited' by colleges for advanced standing in award-bearing provision. United Kingdom FE colleges and the NCVQ need to tackle the accreditation issues in order to avoid the emergence of an 'alternative' training system.

OPENING TIMES

However flexible the NVQ training system looks on paper, with its levels and links and acceptance of prior achievements, the reality may be very different. What impedes flexibility most is local delivery arrangements: the major mismatch between colleges and industry/ commerce is the working year, in the former still 38 weeks (of which two are for administration) and in the latter something like 48 to 50 weeks.

The college argument has been that employers do not want training in August (or presumably July, early September, late December, Easter week, etc) because they go on holiday, although there is no evidence to suggest that businesses close down during the 16 weeks when colleges do not traditionally train. In any event, private trainers continue to work, as do college companies – and some colleges (though usually only with skeletal staff presence).

The academic session is a peculiar anachronism which derives historically from practices employed in universities and public schools. It is perhaps defensible for young children, but why those old enough to join the workforce should be considered capable of working for up to 50 weeks a year but not of learning formally for more than 36 (24 in Oxbridge) is difficult to explain.

In the UK all indications suggest that the traditional academic calendar is on its way out, at least in public sector colleges. Current efforts to renegotiate college management conditions of service to include (a minimum of) only 30 days' annual leave point towards an extended college year. In Australia comparable arrangements already operate among college principals in some states and the declared longer-term objective is to move similar changes downwards through the hierarchy.

What movement towards a 46-week college year has not yet confronted is the problem of increased evening work and of Saturday and Sunday opening. Once the college system attempts widescale training, reskilling and updating of employed adults, it must come up against a variety of reasons why all adults cannot fit easily into conventional weekday slots. For example, contrary to popular teacher belief, the course fee is not necessarily the main training cost for employers. Far more expensive are the opportunity costs: reduced through-put capacity, difficulty in meeting deadlines, the prospect of turning away business. Anything which takes key people out of the office or workshop during the working week is a cost many employers find difficult to meet. Also, in any organisation (business or college) the most dispensable (for part or all of a day) members of the workforce are usually senior managers and very junior staff. Those in between, who represent the majority of people who need reskilling and updating, are often less easy to release from work without disastrous consequences because they carry responsibility for routine operational activity, the bread-and-butter side of the enterprise.

As noted above, the growth of small businesses means that a larger proportion of potential adult customers (and those often most in need of help) are not available during conventional business hours. If they are to receive training at all, it will have to occur in the evening and at weekends. Others who may need more flexible hours are the increasing numbers of single parents, and those families where the man and woman share the child-rearing responsibilities equally.

Even in larger firms, as we move towards 1992 and a more competitive market, the need for increased productivity and reduced costs will create pressure to cut unnecessary expenditure. Training is often the first economy to be made, particularly if it is offered in forms and at times which disrupt business.

In any case the concept of conventional business hours is changing, particularly in retailing. Lunchtime closures have been on the way out for years. Bank Holiday opening by shops is fairly common. Extended day opening is increasing. Despite the failure of the Government's Sunday Trading Bill, more and more shops are opening on Sundays. The result is growth in flexi-time working, which restricts trainee availability. A further complication is that international markets obliterate ordinary timekeeping. We are currently considering a single clock for the whole of the European Community. What will happen when the consolidated Northern workday comes into conflict with the Latin siesta remains to be seen. Those who work in the Tokyo/London/New York money markets already have to be available (despite local Bank Holidays) when customers want to buy and sell.

Our competitors are aware (and have been for years) of the implications. In North America, Summer School is a decades-old service. In many American community colleges, the opening hours are 8 am to 10 pm for teaching, with the library available until 11 pm to allow students at least an hour to use its facilities after formal learning has ceased. Weekend courses represent a growth area.

If more UK adults are to receive training, their courses will more and more have to be matched to customer availability. This availability depends less and less on an entire nation working on a standard work-day and work-year. The need for lifelong education and training moves us inexorably towards year-long and week-long provision.

FLEXIBLE STARTING ARRANGEMENTS

One major consequence of a longer training year must be a movement towards more than a single annual starting date, a traditional characteristic of public sector provision which most fully undermines any pretence of responsiveness. At the beginning of 1989, for example, in a middle-sized English city a secretary wanting to start a shorthand course could do so for a fee of £33 at a local college, or £230 with a well-known private trainer. Apart from cost, the main difference was that the private provider could offer immediate tuition, but the college could accept no new students until September.

Delayed training-starts in UK public-sector colleges have been one of the main stimuli to the growth of private-sector training. What many colleges do not often enough appreciate is that they are no longer in a monopoly position and that most (60 per cent in a national survey, Theodossin, 1989) employers who use college provision also use private trainers.

There are valid reasons why the new adult customer is less likely to fit into traditional college-start arrangements.

1　School leavers have come from an 11-year experience fitted into an academic session beginning in September and ending in July. Adults work calendar years. The idea that a need identified in January cannot be met until September makes no sense to an adult customer.

2　Turning away people for months is a great demotivator. If a sale is to be concluded, the exchange must occur while the customer is still interested. Enough time will dull most people's enthusiasm.

3　When an employer needs workers with particular skills, he or she needs them *now* if marketing opportunities are to be seized. Delayed starts lose sales.

4　Once APLA provision is in place, there can be absolutely no justification for starting accredited customers with advanced entry at the same time as those who lack comparable skills – or in asking the skilled to wait for the others to catch up.

Flexible starts are a challenge to managers. A commitment to facilitating devices (APL, modularisation, credit transfer, etc.) is implicit in the work of NCVQ, but at college level there is a need to translate that commitment into day-to-day operational arrangements, eg equally flexible teacher contracts, extended plant use, increased support staff and (someone's nightmare) the timetable.

Policy and principle are easy enough to encompass rhetorically, but at the practical level they require skilled and imaginative management.

VARIABLE TRAINING VENUES AND MODES

Accepting the idea that people can and do learn outside training establishments has an interesting corollary, that learning can be planned to take place in other venues. Some does, but as with many imported ideas, high-level advocacy is not always followed by chalkface practice. There can be valid reasons.

On a recent trip to Australia, I witnessed highly developed co-operative arrangements where organised adult learning was shared between college and workplace and run jointly by teachers and employers. The impetus was necessity: a small, isolated community with three major industries (accounting for 80 per cent of college business) and difficulties in attracting workers (in another guise, students). In such a situation the college has an important role to play in creating 'new' workers from the existing workforce.

Conviction rather than necessity underlies the achievements of distance learning in Australia. There is both historical and political commitment to make available to people in the outback – often hundreds of miles from the coastal towns – the same kinds of educational and training opportunities provided for the urban population. For the past 15 years the larger states have set up and run external studies units which have well-developed stocks of materials and (more important) buoyant demand. Recently there have been developments in the use of satellites to beam programmes to learners and a movement towards genuine mixed-mode study, part at home and part in college.

To what extent can such practices ever become commonplace in the UK? The recent Open College failure to attract adequate numbers of private students suggest that even with careful marketing it is not always possible to stimulate demand for some services. It also raises questions about why we so often think in terms of exclusive delivery modes, instead of moving towards the development of full-time, part-time and distance, in-plant and college learning as alternative approaches to be assembled as appropriate by individuals.

TRAINING AND ENTERPRISE COUNCILS

All of the above derives from the assumption that college customers are individuals, either students or employers. Usually they are, but not always. There are also brokers. The recent impact of the

Manpower Services Commission (later Training Agency) on colleges shows just how powerful and influential intermediaries can be: they can offer access to lucrative training contracts and their funding can make the difference between austere survival and secure comfort. The currently evolving Training and Enterprise Councils (TECs) are likely to impact with no less force than their predecessor on the worlds of both NVQ and college training, not least because the Training Agency influence and experience will be carried over.

TECs will be independent companies (about 80 in England and Wales), in most cases limited by guarantee. They will be directed by business leaders, have an average of 50 staff and a £20 million budget.[4] Each TEC will be able to establish incentive pay systems and bonuses for exemplary performance.

The intention is that TECs should:[5]

1 promote more effective training by employers and individuals through the use of public programmes and private funds;
2 provide practical help to employers wishing to improve their training efforts;
3 deliver and develop youth training;
4 develop Employment Training under contract with the government;
5 improve the local enterprise and training system so that individuals and firms have easy access to the information and help they need;
6 stimulate business education partnerships.

Thus, from a college perspective, TECs will be powerful brokers whose support will need to be cultivated and whose business will have to be won.

How TECs will in practice function remains to be seen. A question mark hovers over the intention to redeploy Training Agency Area Office staff in the TECs: it is clear that the emphasis on incentive schemes is designed to assist with turning ex-civil servants accustomed to public-sector protection into committed entrepreneurs. However this works out in practice, TECs will have to be taken into account in college NVQ marketing.

WELCOMING CUSTOMERS

Attracting potential customers into the college is one thing. Sustaining their interest is another. The sheer squalor of some college reception areas and teaching facilities becomes apparent only through comparison with overseas provision. Study visits in recent years to Denmark, the United States and Australia have provided me with vivid contrasts of physical plant.

The best of the foreign equivalent of FE colleges are clean and attractive. Carpeted public areas are usual. Furniture and equipment are modern, even contemporary. Decorative features include plants, sophisticated lighting and (often student) artwork. The standard of cleaning is high. The buildings are regularly decorated (some of ours have not been for decades).

Even outside our large cities, college parking arrangements can challenge driver visitors, with the most convenient areas reserved for senior staff, and customers left to prowl, shark-like, for vacant spaces. Not all buildings are adequately heated in the winter. Unrepaired broken windows are not unknown. The worst of the security arrangements would, in the business world, close a shop within days. And so on . . .

If most customers need to come to the college for most of their learning, they require congenial settings. Our college buildings are not only largely old stock (some date from between the wars, many were built more that 20 years ago) but they have generally fared badly in recent educational cutbacks: the politics of local authority college management have ensured that teaching posts have been protected at the expense of support staff posts, so that cleaning, repairs, upkeep and decorating have suffered. In the meantime, the physical standard of living of many of the workforce has improved: public buildings, houses and cars now commonly exhibit refinements which would have been exceptional a few years ago. Colleges are often in the business of trying to attract into slum settings adult customers who tolerate such conditions neither at home nor at work.

Nor is customer care conspicuously present in our colleges. Telephonists and receptionists (often the same person) are still untrained, overworked and badly paid. The result is that at the crucial point of initial customer contact, colleges are most vulnerable and inadequate. For many potential trainees, entering a large bureaucratic institution would in itself be daunting, even if their reception and the physical setting were welcoming.

It is to be hoped that following the devolved financial control which took place in April 1990 colleges will be able to remedy some of their worst deficiencies. However brilliantly planned the new system of vocational qualifications, unless initial customer contacts are improved and the physical plant made more attractive, no amount of advertising and promotion is likely to increase the demand for training among much of the adult workforce.

COUNSELLING SERVICES

Any college which is genuinely concerned with the well-being of its customers will want to make sure that what they purchase is suited to their needs. If the college is to meet the requirements of both students and employers, it ought to consider the following.

1 Before selling a course to a potential student, as part of the standard transaction process, the college should evaluate the student's abilities and achievements. With adults, assessment of prior learning ought to be a routine rather than a requested service.
2 Unlike school leavers, adults are not necessarily looking for a job. Many, in fact, are concerned not with doing their present job better[6] but with using new qualifications to get better jobs. Someone in the college ought to be able to offer advice about whether proposed study/training is likely to lead to the anticipated end, ie to know the local employment scene and the market-place value of the qualifications the college offers.
3 Adult learners are mobile, for which reason they may be unable to complete long courses. When this happens, what advice can be given about transfer arrangements, either to other colleges or other courses or a distance learning mode?
4 Where work or domestic commitments interfere with training, to whom can the student turn for assistance with organising alternative delivery arrangements?
5 Businesses (like students) have training needs, and if the college is to respond to training requirements in the community it will have to consider TNA (discussed above).
6 In the case of small businesses, which can be expected to spend only limited sums on training, it will be necessary for colleges to undertake their own market research to determine what *general* local needs are in order to offer appropriate short courses aimed at a huge market of small enterprises.

Adult customers can be expected to confront counselling staff with a rather different range of problems.

QUALITY: A CUSTOMER PERSPECTIVE

A recurrent challenge in marketing involves accepting that customer and provider perceptions often vary, not merely because they view the experience differently, but also because their needs are not always congruent: the demands of delivering an NVQ cannot be the same as those of training on it.

In open system terms, all the above marketing problems derive from input concerns, ie attracting customers to the new qualifications by informing them of course availability; delivering training at convenient times and in appropriate modes and venues; and getting purchasers to the point of closing a sale. If we were dealing with cars or furniture or clothes we might be able to argue (some would disagree) that the transaction was completed. With education and training, we have only begun. Courses are delivered not only at fixed dates and in published formats and places, but also over time (anything from hours to years). A systems approach requires us to confront through-put or process.

The NCVQ is formally concerned only with the outcomes of the learning process rather than with the character of that process. The process is the college's responsibility. From a national perspective, the arrangement makes good practical and political sense. For students, however, such demarcations have little meaning. Just as restaurant diners seldom distinguish between the relative quality of the cooking and the raw food – and are likely to blame or praise the chef rather than the farmer or the distributor – so with course purchasers. In the long chain of sub-contracting which underlies most provision, individual suppliers may be only too aware of the differences between means and ends, but customers do not often experience them separately.

So, too, with the process itself, which for a customer is both content *and* teachers. Where what the student is learning relates to a job currently held, effectiveness within the workplace is a more powerful judge of appropriateness than the eventual endorsement of a national agency, however rigorous its consultation process.

Nor can the syllabus stand on its own in a taught course: for the learner, teaching is often the major means of mastering content. Having lured the adult student from the workplace into the classroom, the college faces a major delivery challenge: teacher credibility. An undetermined number of FE teachers remain cut off from the workshop or office by lack of contact over many years (decades in some instances). The resulting problems are easier to disguise with inexperienced youngsters, but anyone currently in a job and coming to a college for updating can be expected to use work itself as a fairly precise measuring instrument. In most colleges a pro-gramme of industrial secondments and regular staff updating will be necessary if adult workers are to be themselves updated through NVQs.

From a customer perspective quality control therefore requires formal arrangements for monitoring student perceptions of content and teaching, and for examining areas of significant discontent with a view to improving delivery where possible.

AN AFTER-SALES SERVICE

And so we come to consequences and results, the outcomes which are the major formal responsibility of NCVQ. At the production end of the open system the perceptions of provider and customer are also likely to vary. A national agency such as NCVQ has the power to ensure quality by monitoring output through a formal assessment procedure. The customer will certainly be concerned with that procedure, but the real market-place value of the qualification gained will be determined not by assessment but by outcomes in a somewhat different sense.

The customer will want to use his or her qualification for some purpose. Whether the goal is achieved will ultimately determine how valuble the acquisition is. That in turn will be influenced by market-place supply and demand. Have skill shortages been filled? If that was what he or she was after, did the student get a job? A new job? A promotion? Did the qualification help with the process? Did the skills acquired prove appropriate and sufficient in the workplace? If not entirely, should recruitment be cut or the programme be altered?

What is thus far missing from the NVQ scenario is any commitment to the market research implicit in after-sales service, to tracking at least some NVQ award-holders in order to determine to what extent the splendid intentions have been realised. Gossip and anecdote cannot replace systematic collection of empirical evidence. The kind of customer care involved in such after-sales activity belongs properly not to NCVQ but to the marketing work of the individual college which alone can determine how effective its training has proved.

In the market-place the customer is the final arbiter: the sale may have been concluded for the supplier at the point where cash changes hands, but the purchaser lives with the consequences. A marketing approach based on meeting customer needs has to be judged by the consequences to individuals – employers and students.

REFERENCES

1 Wigan Foundation for Technical Education, *Marketing PICKUP* (The Professional, Industrial and Commercial Updating Programme) WFTE, 1985, ISBN: 0 946629 41 2.

2 NCVQ, *The National Council for Vocational Qualifications in England, Wales and Northern Ireland, Its Purposes and Aims*, 1987.
3 NCVQ, *The National Vocational Qualification Framework*, 1987.
4 Training Agency *Training and Enterprise Councils: a prospectus for the 1990s*, 1989.
5 Training Agency, *A Challenging Role for British Business*, 1989.
6 Theodossin, Ernest, *Marketing the college*, FESC/HMSO, 1989, ISBN: 0 907659 59 4.

Part 2:
New deals with employers

4. NVQs, further education, and the Training and Enterprise Councils (TECs)

Michael Rowarth

INTRODUCTION

The overhead foil showed the National Training Task Force (NTTF) and the National Council for Vocational Qualifications (NCVQ) side by side. The occasion was the induction of the NTTF into the philosophy of the White Paper *Employment for the 1990s*. The point being made was that the proposals for locally established Training and Enterprise Councils (TECs) were positioned within an existing and developing framework of vocational qualifications seen as vital to the future health of training within the UK.

It is easy to be cynical about training (and this chapter will concentrate on the training rather than the enterprise aspects of TECs). After all, our record can hardly be regarded as exemplary. The statistics demonstrate forcibly that we do not yet compare favourably with those industrialised nations whose economic performance we would wish to emulate. Why should the new proposals afford any greater optimism? Business in general has hardly shown its support for training and yet the White Paper is requiring TECs to be led by private sector business. So what's different?

Well, far be it from me to underestimate the power of the vested interest or the inertia of bureaucracy in stopping the progress of NVQs, TECs or any other initiatives but I believe the current training situation is different from that of any other period since 1945. Previous government initiatives such as the 1964 Industrial Training Act have been top-down operations. This time it is a bottom-up approach. Never before have £3 billion, plus operational staff, been given by any government for the local development of training and enterprise via locally driven, private-sector-led corporate bodies independent of both local and national government. Of course there are strings attached: it is public money and there has to be accountability. Of course there is supervision by the Training Agency as the vehicle for that accountability. But there is a new willingness in government to give real freedom for TECs to seize local opportunities unfettered by restrictive historical or Civil Service thinking. If that freedom is not a reality the local high-powered business people who form the TEC boards will abandon the concept *en masse* and the experiment will founder. UK Limited cannot afford that to happen. So where does that leave NCVQ and those who will deliver training, in particular further education (FE), which is a major provider of external training for industry?

NCVQ AND TECs

First, NCVQ is very firmly linked in with the overall plan. The rationalising and the modularising of qualifications are major elements of the NVQ strategy, seen as critical steps in the preparation for future development in training. Not only will employers, parents, pupils and students be able to see the relative value of the plethora of qualifications, they will also have easier access via, for example, modularisation or NVQ units. More specifically for TECs, their money supply will be linked to quality training – and the definition of quality includes the provision of NVQs. The importance of a qualified workforce underlines the thinking of the White Paper, and the only acceptable qualifications (at least for all but the highest levels of qualification) will be those which have the 'kitemark' of the NCVQ.

There are very significant implications for FE in all of this, as regards both broad principle and specific operational detail. Let us look first at the areas of broad principle. A system such as that of NVQs which demystifies and makes simple that which was complicated inevitably undermines the powerbase of those with a vested interest in maintaining the status quo. Certain parts of the legal profession are unhappy about changes which give solicitors access to what was the sole preserve of barristers; banks become concerned about the intrusion into their business of building societies – examples are numerous. Further education colleges find themselves in a similar position. At one time they were the almost exclusive external providers of education and training for local industry and commerce. 'Night School' was the recognised route; day release took over; short courses and block release were added.

Over the past 15 years, however, the quasi-monopoly has begun to crumble at the edges. The MSC, as it was then, has encouraged the growth of the private provider of training and the development of company training departments usually based on large firms – and a new industry has developed. Local centres for examining bodies such as City and Guilds which were not based in FE colleges, were relatively few in number at one time. These non-FE college local centres are increasing rapidly and are now based not only on local firms but on private training providers. The qualifications they offer now extend beyond City and Guilds and include BTEC and Pitman qualifications among many others. NCVQ's activities of demystification and the creation of units will add further impetus to the break-up of the FE quasi-monopoly.

So much for the broad issues. The specific implications of NCVQ for colleges are gradually unfolding as the examination system becomes NVQ 'kitemarked'. So far, any major impact has been absorbed by this process of assimilation. What is abundantly clear is that both staff development and institutional development are critical. Modularisation, for example, implies significant changes in teaching strategy. The issues of access and individualised learning become high on the agenda and they in turn have an impact on the resource base in colleges.

At Newcastle College we have tried in a number of ways to grasp the nettle of the student-centred learning which NCVQ requires. First, we have established a regime of staff–student ratios which allows as much freedom as possible for creative solutions to individualised and small-group learning without increasing demands on staffing. To make this regime work, however, we have had to invest significant sums of money in developing areas suitable for student-centred learning to take place. It is no use cramming students into libraries and expecting results.

Second, therefore, we have taken a floor in each of two teaching blocks and redesigned them to accommodate the new Learning Strategies. Dividing walls have disappeared, reception areas have sprung up, refurbishment and redecoration has created a totally un-college-like environment. High tech access has been facilitated. But however much money is invested in development of this sort, nothing will change unless staff are part of the development.

Since medieval times teachers have been the fount of all knowledge, with students sitting (metaphorically if not literally) at their feet. They have been regarded as sacrosanct figures in the classroom, their superiors in the hierarchy virtually excluded unless permitted by the individual teacher to intrude. That culture has been gradually changed over the years but many lecturers still need help in adapting to, say, team-teaching, and they will certainly need help in coming to terms with learning (as opposed to teaching) in which the student dominates and the lecturer becomes the enabler or the catalyst. To be a servant requires a humility not always found in the classroom prima donna who enjoys the semi-theatrical limelight. So there needs to be a change of attitude and a learning of the skills of the enabler. The skills require sensitivity to individual need quite different from the sensitivity to group needs. The process changes, too, from being dominated by knowledge-transmission to one of learning together.

The learning demanded by NCVQ requires change; so does the content. The curriculum must be modularised in such a way that each module, while standing discretely on its own, must also be capable of easy interlocking with other modules, of providing a foundation on which the next building block can be placed. But, if one has the needs of the self-learning situation in mind, some at least of those modules must also be capable of self-study in which only occasional reference needs to be made to a supervisory lecturer. Staff will therefore have to learn to identify such modules, adapting them where necessary to their particular circumstances; they will need to learn quick and reliable ways of assessing that learning has taken place to a point which allows the lecturer and student to proceed either in an individual or a group situation. The writing of learning programmes has thus become part of our staff development for those staff involved in our student-centred learning areas.

Staff development for NCVQ should not stop with academic staff, of course. It involves library staff who have an important part to play in the development of the individual's learning skills, in the building up of information packs, in the creation of information retrieval systems which accommodate the spirit of the modular approach in a positive way. Administrative staff also are a key element in the easy access approach which NCVQ and modularisation demand. The switchboard, the receptionist, the porter, all play a significant rôle in smoothing the way into the college and their development is as important as that of the enabling lecturer.

This is a huge canvas of activity to be covering and I would not pretend that we have covered all of it yet – but we in Newcastle College and in FE generally have made a promising start. We are beginning to be aware that the NCVQ approach is going to make demands on us in learning strategies, in accommodation require-ments, in the distribution of resources, in the development of staff throughout our college structures. We are beginning to be aware, too, that NCVQ may accelerate the development of the private provider and the company training department, so that they can compete in every way with FE. The monopoly, if such it ever really was, can now be seen to be in the process of being dismantled, and competition will increase.

That competitive aspect of the field of training has already had implications for FE. Marketing is well known within FE as a concept now, but it is still rather crude and unsophisticated and much has to be learned from industry and commerce on how to market effectively. But the will is there and FE learns fast. Following April 1990 when the Education Reform Act has begun to bite that learning process will accelerate.

Into this scene of uncertainty, competition and increasing development steps the Training and Enterprise Council. What is it? How will it affect the local training and education providers? What will its relationship be with NCVQ? Should we fear it or welcome it? Let's start from the beginning.

TECs AND FURTHER EDUCATION

In facing up to the comparatively poor performance of UK training, the government has been anxious to identify the reasons for the better performance of our industrialised competitors. The attractions of the German system led to an examination of the potential of Chambers of Commerce to develop into the local agencies for training. However, it would seem that while some excellent work was being carried out in training by certain Chambers, not all were capable of the speedy development needed to cope with the problem. The United States had, however, produced a model which offered a possible way forward: the Private Industry Councils (PICs). These have been in operation for about ten years and originally were seen as being led by an equal partnership of local government and local business. However, in the early 1980s, employers were given the lead rôle. There are now 600 PICs. Most are linked in with local government but the rest - something under a third - either are (or act like) corporate bodies. It is this latter model which has proved attractive to the government and has been adopted for the TECs. The first point for colleges to note therefore is that the TECs are businesses limited by guarantee.

It is one thing, of course, to have a model, but quite another to have support for that model from the people one is trying to involve. When TECs were first mooted there was considerable scepticism voiced about the response from industry for yet another initiative which called on their time and resources. The world of business, it was said, was already being asked to contribute so much to work placements for the Youth Training Scheme (YTS), and to collaboration with schools in the Technical and Vocational Education Initiative (TVEI) and with Compacts. Industry Year had exerted further pressure for businesses to get involved with local education institutions, as had Sir Adrian Cadbury's Report on Business and Schools: all this in addition to long-established involvement with education, for example, in the provision of work experience, the funding of research work and professorial chairs. There had to be a limit to what the business world could give and TECs would make demands beyond that limit. That has not proved to be the case.

TECs require that at least two-thirds of the Board should be top business leaders from the private sector who are chairmen, chief executives or the top operational managers at local level of major companies. They should reflect the mix of local industry and include small businesses. 'Impossible! How will the top people spare the time? In any case they don't know anything about training,' has been the cry. But the doubters have so far been confounded. More than double the expected number of submissions for approval were received in the first tranche. In those 22 submissions the number of problems related to the status of the Board membership were miniscule and those problems were solved very quickly. In my capacity as a Task Force member reviewing the submissions for approval, I have been really impressed by the enthusiasm of the business community to get to grips with the issues of training and enterprise in their locality. I have been impressed, too, by the breadth of their vision and their willingness to spread the TEC influence as widely as possible and necessary. They have seen the need for the social implications to be properly explored, for the relationships not only with training providers but also with schools to be developed and for TECs not to be mere Area Training Offices under a new name. So if the first lesson was that TECs are businesses limited by guarantee, the second lesson for colleges to learn is that the private sector members of the TEC Boards have real commitment and real vision.

The third lesson for colleges is that TEC Boards will not, *in the first instance*, have any direct jurisdiction over TVEI, Compacts, Work Related Further Education or Enterprise in Higher Education. I believe we have not heard the end of this particular matter. A battle over the inclusion of these areas within the TEC remits has been won or lost, depending on where you stand, but there is no final victory in this war as yet. Indeed, the CBI response to the TEC initiative indicates that TECs 'must have an overview' over the education provision indicated above and states, 'There is a strong argument that TECs should have a degree of direct responsibility for at least some of the vocational education initiative' currently within the education sector. It will not be long, I think, before the influence of TECs within schools and colleges becomes powerful.

Let us pause a moment to examine this. As far as schools are concerned, TECs will be concerned about the number of school children available for recruitment to industry, especially in areas of skill shortage. The demographic trend will make this a matter of some urgency. TECs will therefore begin to liaise with schools not only on TVEI and Compact matters, but on wider issues of general attainment and they will wish to see that pupils are achieving in NVQ terms so that they can progress more easily into programmes of vocational education and training when they leave school. Indeed, if TECs heed the CBI report they will be pressing schools that their 16-19-year-old pupils should all be 'embarked upon courses of study or training combined with work experience leading to attainment of NVQ Level II or equivalent by 1995'. The relationship between TECs and schools will be smoothed by the increased business representation on school governing bodies and by the greater freedom which schools will have in negotiations with bodies such as TECs following the Education Reform Act.

If TECs see themselves involved with and in schools – and they will – how much more will that apply to colleges which have been involved so deeply with educating and training for industry and commerce since their early beginnings in Mechanics Institutes. Although the greatest single programme in colleges is that related to GCSE and GCE A Level studies, the majority of the remainder of college work is business-linked. Over the past few years, colleges have been encouraged via PICKUP and such projects as the Responsive College, to market themselves to industry and commerce in a way they have never done before. Incentive has been added by the demographic trend which, although it so far has had no effect on numbers within FE establishments, represents a threat of student reductions.

A further incentive to build stronger links with industry is the financial base of FE, which is vulnerable from the reducing budgets of local authorities, the disinclination of local authorities to invest in institutions they fear will go the way of the polytechnics, and the replacement of traditional full-time FE students by short course and part-time students who do not attract the same level of funding.

So historically and currently FE is locked into the local economy in a way which will demand the attention of TECs. What will be the consequence of that attention? Clearly nobody can yet tell but various scenarios present themselves. The first is that of controller of FE in an area or a region. The second is that of a training provider to carry out the TEC programme with the various conditions attached, including the NVQ dimension.

First, let us look at TEC as the controller of Further Education. We know that Work Related FE forms a large part of any FE college provision and that that is already effectively directed by the Department of Employment through the local Training Agency Office. We know, too, that TECs will be concerned about levels of attainment of young people across the board and about the supply of young as well as older people to help some skill shortage problems. It is but a short step for colleges to come directly under the control of TECs and this would be seen as a logical step by many. If that came about then the role the Regional Advisory Councils never really adopted (nor have been expected to adopt) would fall to the TECs. They would decide exactly where provision would be located and would, as appropriate, rationalise FE.

That scenario may have attractions for some but it probably would not attract many TEC Boards. They would prefer not to have the management and administrative responsibility for colleges. The burden of direct control would outweight the advantages. It would be far better for colleges to be simply a source of training provision, whether they are inside or outside the control of local authorities.

Let us turn to the second possibility therefore: colleges as training providers. There would seem to be little difference in the relationship between colleges and the Training Agency, and colleges and TECs. After all, TECs will be responsible for the YTS and ET programmes as well as Business Growth Training (BGT), which is basically existing provision rationalised under a new title. Nothing much will have changed perhaps. My observations of the TEC teams that have come forward so far is that, although some will move more swiftly than others, there will be significant developments in local training and enterprise as a result of the formation of TECs. If there isn't, why bother? Certainly, none of the top businessmen recruited to date will stay with a rubber-stamping role which ensures the current programmes are carried out but under another administrative framework. Some of them have already indicated the need for attitude-change training for Civil Servants who are moving from the Training Agency office to the TECs, and that seems to me to be indicative of a desire to ensure there is a far-reaching change of approach.

What, then, will the changes be? Initially TECs will need to find their feet and the first year or so (from April 1990 for the first TECs) will see a period of settling in. YTS and ET will continue, although we should note the influence demographic changes and high levels of employment especially in the South East will have on YTS. We should also take note of talk within the Treasury about clawing back YTS monies as the numbers available for schemes fall.

During this settling in period the TECs will be anxious to follow the aims set out in the Strategic Guidance document, *Training and Enterprise: Priorities for Action 1990/91*, which are:

1 to help businesses improve their performance by encouraging them to plan and undertake training to achieve clear business aims;
2 to help ensure that young people acquire the skills the economy needs;
3 to help ensure that unemployed people, and particularly the long-term unemployed, acquire the skills, experience and enterprise to help them find and keep a job;
4 to encourage new businesses to start and existing businesses to grow;
5 to help make the providers of vocational education aware of local labour market needs and to promote links between education and employers;
6 to improve the training system by ensuring there is an effective local, sectoral and national framework.

The examination of these aims will establish the way in which colleges can relate to TECs in the future, should they so wish. It would be difficult to imagine a college which would not wish to be involved but there is, of course, no requirement that they should be. What process does a college need to follow?

ACTION FOR COLLEGES

The first step for a college (or group of colleges within one LEA), after examining the TEC aims, is to determine within its own overall planning whether it wishes to relate to TEC. Assuming it does, it then needs to write to the TEC Board (or the Steering Group if there is as yet no approved Board) to indicate its desire to be involved and to seek discussion with Members of the Board on an informal basis. Such a discussion would help to establish what the ethos of the Board is and it would be particularly important that before those discussions the college should have sight of any documents which the TEC could make available, especially the application for development funding to the National Training Task Force, which will give details of the Board members' employment history, the TEC organisation, its geographical area, indication of support from the business community, its priorities for change and improvement, and the proposed budget for and the organisation of the development work. This may be the only document immediately available but colleges should not be afraid of asking for it (or any other papers) as there is a requirement for TECs to communicate and to consult with the local community. The *Draft Operating Manual* for TECs shows that each TEC 'will [not only] publish a synopsis of its agreed annual Business Plan . . . [but that] the process by which a TEC develops and publicises the Business Plan will provide an important means of communicating its Strategic Objectives and approach to training and enterprise.' It is worth pursuing this requirement on TECs to communicate and consult for it provides the key by which colleges (and others, of course) can open the door into TECs. Colleges may find a TEC establishes 'task forces of interest groups to advise on key issues related to programme design features and performance outcomes', and clearly colleges could make a significant contribution to such task forces by becoming members. Apart from any such initiatives TECs will publish Annual Reports and hold public meetings. Colleges will want to be aware of both these methods of keeping in touch.

Let us return to the discussions between a college and the TEC Board. The structure of the Boards is such that the Board itself may delegate much of its operational work to sub-groups which may be concerned with, say, young people or the unemployed, business growth or the employed. Thus, it may be appropriate for discussion to take place with some or all of these sub-groups or their chairmen or – women. These sub-groups, incidentally, are likely to include one or two Board members but will be made up mainly of people at a level lower than chief executive. Many will be personnel specialists and will know their way round the training scene.

However, colleges should not assume that their work will be well-known (or known at all) by either the Board or its sub-groups. It would be helpful therefore for colleges to be prepared to sell themselves relatively hard as other training providers will do. A presentation may be appropriate, a visit to a college campus, a package of information – or all three. Whatever is done, the important message is that colleges need to establish their track record with TECs. Do not assume that the business which came before through the Training Agency will automatically come again.

Having made contact, a college should maintain it. The first contact will need follow-up. Officials currently in post at the Training Agency may know a college well but the college should not rely on them to promote its cause. Those officials will no longer be working for the Training Agency and will probably have a different job within a TEC.

Lest I have created the impression that colleges will be at a disadvantage with TECs and that TECs will sweep away the old order and install a new one which will be private-sector based to the exclusion of colleges, let me reassure them. TECs are going to need all the help they can get from wherever they can get it. They have a massive job to do and those members of TEC Boards I have met so far have recognised the awesome responsibility they have taken on. They know they have much to learn whether it be about NVQs (and I believe the NCVQ perhaps through the professional associations has a job to do here in educating Board Members in what NVQs are all about) or about Training Agency programmes, about training providers or about skill shortages. Colleges have a part to play not only in providing the training but in sharing their achievements to date and demonstrating their potential for the future. There is absolutely no doubt that TECs will need colleges to help them achieve their ambitious aims.

Acquiring the skills the economy needs

The first of those aims to be of direct importance for colleges is 'To help ensure that young people acquire the skills the economy needs.' The purpose of this is:

1 To re-establish the government's guarantee of a suitable training place for all 16 and 17 year olds not in a job or full-time education. (Colleges will continue to play their part as they have done to date. No real change.)

2 To help ensure that everyone under 19 has the chance to attain a qualification at least at NVQ Level 2 or equivalent. (The implications for colleges are clear. Within the academic policy there will need to be clear reference to this aim and to how the college proposes to achieve it through its existing and future programmes. Before implementation, however, comes the staff development in NVQs which has been referred to earlier.)

3 To increase the proportion of young people obtaining qualifications at higher skill levels. (Again, colleges will need to assimilate this within their academic policy and determine the implications for their programmes.) There will be at least two aspects to this: (i) increasing the number of students by including those who would not normally continue their education beyond school (one way to raise the percentage of people obtaining qualifications at higher skill levels than they would normally attain); and (ii) raising the expectations of those who would come into colleges anyway, so that they achieve at a higher level than they might

otherwise have expected to reach. There is clearly a limit to the number who will achieve beyond their normal expectation, but there will be some, and attention needs to be paid therefore to methods of selection and to teaching and learning strategies to help those who have the potential.

4 To increase the proportion of young people entering further and higher education. (Colleges are only one factor to be taken account of in this area: schools, parents, employers, and government funding policies all have an effect on this issue.) Nevertheless colleges can do more through improving their marketing and the services they offer students.

5 To ensure that training and vocational education complement and support each other in every locality. Colleges have much to offer in the achievement of this aim. They need to establish themselves within the TEC framework as the key partners in vocational education, to be those to whom TECs will automatically turn when seeking help to ensure that what happens in training and what happens in education interlock.

6 To ensure that the particular needs of disadvantaged young people are met. Many colleges are already well versed in helping this group. It is up to them to ensure TECs know what they do, and to offer their expertise in developing opportunities for these special young people within the TEC regime. Colleges are particularly well placed to help TECs in this area and they should make the running.

Ensuring the unemployed acquire skills

The second goal of TECs which affects colleges directly is: 'To help ensure that unemployed people, and particularly the long-term unemployed, acquire the skills, experience and enterprise to help them find and keep a job.' Colleges have much experience with the unemployed and the value of that experience to TECs should not be underrated. The purpose of this TEC goal is:

1 'To help ensure that training leads wherever possible to a recognised qualification or a credit towards one.' Colleges involved in Employment Training (ET) have an opportunity and responsibility to exert their influence so that in their locality everyone expects all ET training to lead to qualifications or credits towards one. The colleges should make a firm stand and should present themselves as the leading experts on qualifications – which they are. However, they need to be certain that NCVQ

philosophy has been absorbed and they are prepared for the implications of NVQs both in institutional and personnel terms.

2 'To help ensure that training meets the needs of local labour markets.' Colleges have as strong a grasp of what the local labour market needs as anybody and much of that need will already be reflected within the Work Related Further Education plan. Colleges need to make TECs aware of this. Colleges need to realise the strength of their position in this area. They have a wide, well-developed network which has been operating over many years. This will not be the only network in existence in the locality – the CBI and Chambers of Commerce will have theirs, too – but it should be seen as a major vehicle in helping to achieve this TEC goal and should be marketed as such.

3 'To meet the special training needs of disadvantaged people.' This develops a previous aim which referred only to young disadvantaged people. Again, colleges are in a unique position to help and should promote their experience and expertise to the TECs.

Encouraging new and existing businesses

The third aim which involves colleges is concerned with encouraging 'new businesses to start and existing businesses to grow'. Colleges' experience in this area varies. Those that are well-established within the small-firm sector should ensure their work is well known to the TECs. Those which are not well versed in this area should give serious consideration to helping with the specific training requirements of small firms. Business growth is not an easy area and it is precisely for that reason that colleges should be seen to be trying to help. It is simple to assist with the comfortable areas but TECs will need all the help they can get in these difficult areas, too. I am not urging that colleges should try to deliver in areas in which they have no experience, but they should show a genuine willingness to try to solve the problems of the more difficult aspects of TEC work. If it turns out that they cannot contribute much (or at all) then so be it – but TECs will genuinely appreciate the desire to be of assistance.

Knowing local labour needs and promoting links with employers

The fourth TEC aim directly affecting Colleges is to 'help make the providers of vocational education aware of local labour market needs and to promote links between education and employers'. Colleges could see themselves as having 'arrived' in this area. They are aware of local market needs and they know only too well the need to promote links between education and employers. They should beware of complacency, however. They should also recognise that their expertise, gathered over many years, may be an asset that can be shared without losing out to the competition. In this totally new scene we have to be prepared to step out in faith and share for the greater good. There is so much training to be done that we really cannot lose.

The concern of this fourth aim is to promote continuity and coherence between education and training for young people and adults. Further Education is in a unique position here for both education and training take place on its premises. Colleges should, therefore, involve themselves with TEC personnel in defining and clarifying what is meant by this priority; in initiating pilot studies; in implementing what seems appropriate as a result of those studies. FE has an enviable record of being responsive. It now needs to take the initiative in a firm and professional way.

The TECs are also concerned here to help develop effective education/business partnerships, especially in deprived areas, to improve the quality and skills of the workforce. Colleges have many employer contacts which schools could find useful. They could identify the most appropriate employers and help to match them with schools. Additionally, colleges could use their TVEI work as a vehicle for pushing this priority along, since that encompasses schools, the colleges, employers and the local education authority. Colleges would naturally have to remember that, as part of the LEA, their role might be a relatively junior one, but they should not be slow to offer their help wherever it seems it could be best used.

The TECs also want to improve the planning of vocational education to ensure that education is relevant to working life, to the needs of adults and to local needs. Although there is potential ambiguity in the way this priority is phrased, it seems to be referring to curriculum planning, not to the planning of provision. That being so, colleges should check their systems which determine that existing courses still meet the needs of the customers and that new courses are properly designed. More of that later.

Finally, this fourth aim wishes to increase the contribution that further and higher education make to the continuing education and training of young people and adults. This needs clarification! But the role of the college is to help the TEC work out what this means for their area. Colleges would obviously want to support this aim, but there are hidden implications regarding such matters as resources for their additional contribution. It is essential, therefore, that colleges are closely involved in working out what this priority means in terms of delivery, content and resources, and then in helping to make it happen.

Improving the training system

The fifth and final TEC aim that directly involves colleges is about improving the training system. Colleges need to understand the thinking behind the statement within this aim which says, 'To ensure that responsibility for training and enterprise is devolved as far as possible to local employer-led groups'. This does not mean private providers rule. It means that the private sector should be given the responsibility for ensuring it happens: not of doing it themselves. They could not carry out all the training required. They are not in business to train but to make a profit and they will, therefore, be looking for training providers who can deliver. Of course they will continue in-company training – and we must hope they will develop it – but just as now they will use sub-contractors: local colleges, training consultants, etc.

Intended within this fifth aim is that everyone dealing with training and enterprise should have access to relevant information. Colleges should not wait for that information but should be asking for it. Having acquired it they should act on it and let the TEC know what they are doing.

'To encourage the development and use of open and flexible learning' is a further concern of this aim, and this priority is one which colleges may feel they can capitalise on. TECs may be willing to fund development work, and if it is the college's academic plan to develop this area of their work (and it should be) they should approach the TEC to see if they can involve themselves in mutually beneficial work. But colleges should take care that they have development of open and flexible learning firmly embedded in their academic thinking. An opportunist approach to the subject will result in disaster.

The final concern of this aim is to encourage the development of a national system of vocational qualifications based on recognised standards accepted by industry. It would be easy for colleges to stand back and let NCVQ, the examining bodies, and industry assume responsibility here. The temptation should be resisted. Colleges should be intimately involved in all the local discussions. Their knowledge is wide and has been accumulated over many years; it spans industrial needs, the requirements of examining bodies, assessment techniques, and teaching and learning strategies. TECs need to know of the invaluable contribution colleges can make to the debate. Colleges should tell them.

The message that colleges have a considerable part to play in helping TECs achieve their aims has, I hope, been received. Colleges should be confident in their ability to deliver: they have much going for them. However, they should not be complacent and there is one major issue in particular that they need to keep before them: quality.

THE IMPORTANCE OF QUALITY

We hear much from industry about the way they keep their competitive edge through focusing on quality. Further Education has much to learn from the private sector here. The businessmen and women serving on TECs will understand the concept of quality, will recognise it when they see it and will be consciously searching for it in the services they are receiving from training providers. To be ensuring quality will be the touchstone for the TECs' success. TECs 'will wish to construe [their] role as the leading edge of local training and enterprise to which others will look for a considered plan for development and for guidance, help, and co-ordination.'[1] If they are to succeed in this role, quality in every part of the TECs' work will be essential. Indeed, a TEC will not only be judged by placement rates and recognised qualifications (ie NVQs) but a 'TEC may also be given a performance bonus for exemplary achievement measured by qualitative factors rather than numerical targets.'[2] The Training Agency will encourage a TEC increasingly to use contracts with programme providers that link funding to results. To achieve those results and thus help TECs achieve their objectives will require providers of quality.

The issue of quality is given full prominence in the *Draft Operating Manual* and written into this is a special section on quality assurance which begins:

> A TEC's overall performance and its capacity to meet its contractual obligations to the Government depend . . . on the performance of the contractors who deliver the programmes on its behalf. For this reason quality control and development are essential functions for every TEC. Each TEC will design its own quality strategy . . . and as part of its commitment to quality, a TEC should pay particular attention to promoting the use of vocational qualifications reflecting standards agreed by industry nationally and accredited by NCVQ.

How colleges can achieve or improve the quality of their provision in anticipation of the arrival of TECs is a very big question which cannot be answered in detail here, but there are two key areas which colleges would do well to review as a start to answering the question for themselves.

The first is academic planning and evaluation. A car manufacturer does not wait for the customer to comment on his product before beginning to think about the quality of his cars. He endeavours to lead them to comment positively by what he does prior to delivery. So should colleges. New courses should be well researched both in terms of market and content before being launched. Existing academic programmes should be evaluated by students, staff and employers on a regular basis to ensure they are delivering against agreed criteria to an identified market. The processes for scrutiny of programmes should be stringent and FE colleges should look to higher education (HE) for guidance, for HE has had much experience of this over many years. Clearly NVQs are going to be highly significant within the performance criteria required by TECs, and colleges would do well to ensure that they are ahead of the field in their knowledge of NVQs and their adoption of the philosophy and the practice.

The second area for colleges to review is that of finance. TECs will be indirectly looking for quality in financial affairs through their desire to achieve the highest quality at the cheapest price. Competitive tendering will be adopted where appropriate. Colleges are not yet as experienced as they will have to be in the areas of costing, budgeting and financial control generally. But they will need to observe that, although TECs not only have the freedom to raise money but are positively encouraged[3] to do so, as the PICs' experience in the United States has not been too positive. According to the LSE research paper, 'TECs and VET',[4] 'The best PICs have been able to raise only 7–8% of their income through private financial support.' All of which means that TECs will be looking for additional monies from savings and, in turn, that means colleges need to look to the quality of their financial management as much as to the quality of their academic programmes.

PROMPTS TO ACTION

The major factors which colleges need to observe and act on relating to Training and Enterprise Councils are:

1 TECs are new and will, in finding their way to achieving their objectives, be glad of any professional help they can get. They will respond to those who are anxious to help and who make approaches accordingly.

2 They are private-sector led and will be looking for providers who

5. Competence and coherence: opportunities for education and industry in the emerging NVQ framework

Lester Greenacre

WHY COMPETENCE?

Both employers and educationalists have found 'competence' strangely difficult to define. This is particularly true of the construction industry with which I work. Here there exists a glaring disequilibrium between those employees who have undergone some formal training and earn their living from the industry, and those (a far greater number) who have received no training at all yet find employment, and ostensibly perform as efficiently.

This situation may derive partly from the historic gulf that has existed between industry and education which has led to the development of two quite different definitions of what competence is, and how it is demonstrated. Competence in educational terms has meant the ability to perform to a given standard in a test, or series of tests, based upon the content of the syllabus in question.

In industrial terms, competence quite simply means the ability to perform a task, or range of tasks, to the standards demanded by the employer. While some variations may be experienced between individual employers in an industry, it has generally been possible to identify an industry 'standard', although standards have tended to emerge from anecdotal rather than statistical information.

So, as long as the syllabus and the industry standards corresponded, there might have been a convergent basis for a competence-based system. However, educational institutions (and here I include schools as well as colleges) may find it difficult or even undesirable to dismantle a system based on timetables and set courses for a whole host of reasons which are entirely understandable. These include lack of adequate resources for developing staff and facilities, the external rigidities imposed by an arcane examination system and, paradoxically, the demands of employers who have come to expect a 'tried and tested' product.

Similarly industry finds itself prone to the fluctuations of the economy which may necessitate retrenchment one year, and wholesale recruitment the next. The construction industry is particularly vulnerable to such stresses and strains. Given the prime requirement to deliver the goods and make a profit, employers understandably find it necessary in time of rapid market expansion to recruit labour at short notice and from previously untrawled waters. Thus, competence on the job may be assessed subjectively by observation, and at worst by anecdotal evidence and a demonstration of a 'lack of incompetence'.

To put it simply, the divergence in perception of competence is evidenced by a 'can he or she pass the test?' on the one hand, to 'can he or she do the job?' on the other, and it is this matching exercise between test and job where the Lead Industry Bodies (LIBs), such as CITB, find some of their major tasks.

Within the construction industry the issues of competence and standards of performance are brought into sharp focus by the unique structure of the industry, the key features of which are:

1 a highly mobile and fragmented workforce;
2 a very large number (in percentage as well as numerical terms) of very small units of production (92 per cent of firms employ fewer than 12 people);
3 susceptibility to peaks and troughs in demand brought about by changes in interest rates and central and local government public-spending policies. This makes long-term manpower planning extremely difficult;
4 an enormously varied range of working environments in which the skills of the workforce are displayed. Climatic, logistical and environmental contexts can change quite rapidly, even on the same site. The implications of such factors for defining standards of competence, and then setting about assessing them in an objective way are obvious;
5 the organisational structure of the industry, whereby work may be sub-contracted to specialist firms several times. The main contractor's rôle may therefore primarily be one of contract management.

Defining standards, and bringing forward models for assessment and delivery of the underpinning skills and knowledge, are tasks which LIBs must approach in collaboration with the deliverers and the users. It is a diagnostic and consultative exercise which, as well as being essential for the definition of common goals in vocational education and training could have far-reaching spin-offs in integrating the curriculum and the economy in a fundamental way.

The CITB model for developing a competence framework

The Construction Industry Training Board (CITB) is involved in defining standards of competence on behalf of and in conjunction with the construction industry. It is a process which necessarily must be wide-ranging and must meet the clearly defined needs of industry while at the same time it must develop deliverable and assessable standards. This requires the involvement of individuals and institutions who will be involved at the sharp end, and the testing and evaluation of hypotheses which are developed in support of a framework of vocational qualifications for the industry.

The first stage has been to identify those competences which the industry regards as being relevant to every definable occupation within it. Representatives from education and training, as well as industry, are involved in the focus groups and the Co-ordinating Committee, and may be participants in the smaller working groups.

Having established what these competences are, groups are then made responsible for identifying sub-groupings of competences which will reflect the needs of industry. In the short term this exercise will be focused on intra-occupational groupings to promote coherence in progression from Level I to Levels III or IV, but in the longer term the review will embrace inter-occupational groupings to facilitate the lateral coherence which was alluded to earlier.

This exercise will also help industry and its awarding bodies to identify where requirements common to all exist, so that competences and elements of competence which are relevant to a number of occupational groups are defined via the same unit. In this way a series of core units will emerge which will certainly make individuals more flexible in the range of tasks they can undertake. Specialist or technical units will then provide the specificity which local employers may require.

This programme must be supported by rigorous and varied assessments. The feasibility of workplace assessment in construction has not yet been fully tested, and it is likely that a range of assessment methods may have to be introduced over a period of time.

The major problem is that the contexts in which site-based competence must be demonstrated are variable, since climate, environmental and organisational factors all combine to make objective assessment of performance very difficult. Employers themselves may find it difficult to assess, and smaller firms in particular may not have the capacity to do so. Consequently the LIBs, awarding bodies, employers and delivering institutions will need to work together to develop flexible assessment methods which produce cost effective and reproducible results across the wide range of working environments.

The ultimate success of this review exercise depends on collaboration. LIBs can provide the forum for dialogue necessary to identify the standards in employment, but there is also a requirement that mechanisms for meeting local market demands while adhering to national standards, are established at an early date.

WHY COHERENCE?

It was perhaps inevitable that an input-led model would lead to a fragmented pattern of training provision. It would be wrong, however, to try to place the responsibility for such fragmentation and incoherence on any one particular party. (At a local level there are a number of shining examples of how education and industry have collaborated to satisfy the needs of the local economy.) Nevertheless there has always been a need for an underpinning framework which was logical, coherent and readily understandable by colleges and employers alike. Without such a structure, problems of credibility (of qualifications), inflexibility (of labour) and inefficiency (in the deployment of both industrial and educational resources) could become endemic.

There is no doubt that inflexibility affected the construction industry earlier than it did in other industrial sectors, mainly because of its peculiar structure. A workforce as mobile as the construction industry's is not easy to satisfy. The frequent movement from site to site is an obstacle to skill development and the individual finds it difficult to plot a career path with any degree of certainty. Uncertain and fluctuating work patterns make attendance at any one institution extremely difficult, and long-duration off-the-job programmes present considerable logistical difficulties.

This difficulty is exacerbated for the mature operative or technician who wishes to expand or extend his or her skills. Many of those employed in this category work for very small companies and are frequently self-employed. For such people it simply is not an option to spend time away from the firm in order to undergo training.

Coherence, then, must be exemplified at two levels:

1 the macro level, at which industry and education can clearly see the national pattern of qualifications so that local programmes can be developed rationally;

2 the micro level, at which individuals can gather parcels of skills (or competences) in a way which is not limited by time or place, but which are consistent with the broader picture.

Accumulation and coherence must enable individuals to develop in a way which is consistent with the job being done at the time. Thus changing job content should be reflected in the choice of competences available, and vertical accumulation (ie within the context of a given occupational field), should be matched by opportunities for lateral accumulation (ie across occupational boundaries or through the identification of a common core of skills for a range of occupations).

It is desirable that new entrants to an industry are credited with skills they have developed elsewhere and are not required to start again from scratch, as is often the case. Not only is this incoherence enormously wasteful of resources, but it is also very demotivating for the individual concerned. There are already plenty of reasons why people of all ages eschew opportunities to develop their skills, and it is therefore incumbent on us all to reduce the number of reasons these folk have for saying 'no'. Demonstrable coherence across and along complete paths would seem to be a major step in this direction.

This concept of coherence is also relevant in integrating pre-vocational work with the vocational, ensuring that schools are brought fully into the system so that the artificial 16-year-old break-point is no longer seen as a developmental start and finish point. The formal accreditation of skills developed on the practical, work-based elements of programmes such as TVEI is both desirable and possible, and should form part of the same coherent path to the world of work and beyond.

WHAT OPPORTUNITIES?

The promotion of competence and coherence within a national framework thus requires liaison between the deliverers and the users of vocational competence. This in itself is a major opportunity. There is still a suspicion, however, among those used to timetables, fixed syllabuses and long-duration off-the-job training, that the light we see in the darkness is not in fact the end of the tunnel but a burglar's torch. The emphasis on outcome-led programmes means that the delivery of training becomes a hugely varied means to an end, and opens the door to all sorts of competition. Are these threats or opportunities?

It is incumbent on LIBs and Awarding Bodies to take these issues into account when they set standards and create assessment mechanisms, and to highlight the many new functions which will need to be developed in order to make the emerging system operate efficiently. These are the opportunities which industry and education must grasp.

It will be possible to meet the needs of the local economy much more accurately, since the range of competences which is being developed for each occupation in each industrial sector will have been agreed as *National* standards, and thus, although the programmes which are delivered will reflect local needs (as many do at the moment), they will carry with them the credibility of being valid anywhere. Furthermore they need not be ends in themselves. Credit accumulation demands that each individual should be able to plan a personal development profile which will grow and develop to meet his or her own changing circumstances as well as the changing demands of the economy.

NVQs cover an area and a level of competence: these are the two axes within the NVQ framework. Thus the potential market for NVQs will expand from the fixed, vertical competence profile, to one where more flexible competence profiles are demanded by employers and individuals alike. In other words, while certain qualifications will be vocationally orientated in their own right, (in construction these will include bricklaying, carpentry and joinery, plant operations, plumbing and so on), it will not be difficult to identify:

1 individuals who by the nature of their job require far fewer competences than the full set;
2 employers who wish to see operatives with a range of skills from each of the occupational groups.

While Lead Industry Bodies can enable these types of outcome to become possible through setting up the national 'menu' on behalf of the industry, local mechanisms will need to be established to capitalise on the opportunities offered. It must be remembered here that the standards which are being defined are those of industry, and it is industry that 'owns' them. If the review process has been properly undertaken by the Lead Industry Body, this sense of ownership will be reflected in an enthusiasm and willingness to collaborate with deliverers, through workplace assessment, accreditation of prior learning and so on.

Achieving NVQ units at Level I will provide a foundation, for advancement, and this will be recognised by industry as having a value in itself for those whose capabilities or aspirations do not extend beyond this level. This foundation may extend across a wide range of trades, such as building and specialist building, or there may be units which serve a number of trades within a given craft area.

The implications for deliverers of such a system will be considerable, since scarce resources can be rationalised more effectively and there will be little or no duplication of 'basic' skill work, as is the case in the existing patterns of training. By resourcing one or two areas it will be possible to meet demands for:

- foundation level awards;
- four or five specialist craft streams which emerge therefrom;
- lateral foundation level mixes of competences for general building, kitchen fitting and so on.

This type of output-led model will also demand an equally flexible selection of delivery mechanisms and delivery methods, since without a means of gaining units from different areas and levels of competence, the whole exercise would become meaningless.

The extent of such a reappraisal will be as comprehensive and wide-ranging as that which Lead Industry Bodies, such as CITB, are currently undertaking on behalf of industry.

This development model will be described later, but given the shared goals of the participants and the common threads which run through these exercises (ie the dialogue with industry, the interests of the certificating and awarding bodies), the Lead Industry Bodies must advise and be sensitive to the messages emerging from these local dialogues. Figure 5.1 exemplifies the wide-ranging requirements of this exercise.

It is evident that the implication of a competence-led system will demand a whole range of delivery mechanisms from which consumers will be able to choose. It may be possible for colleges to identify clearly a range of 'products' which meet the local market, while we must be realistic and acknowledge that resource limitations may determine the range which particular colleges can offer.

There are apects of this emerging choice which will be more demanding of college resources than others. These will include:

- diagnosing prior achievement and advising on appropriate routes through the range of competences;
- accrediting such achievements and liaising with awarding bodies;
- assessing in the workplace;
- delivering learning in the workplace.

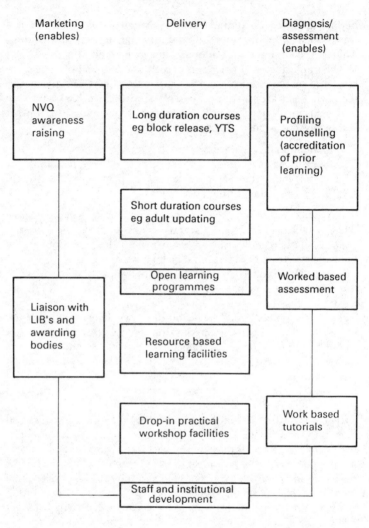

Figure 5.1 *Delivery review process for FE*

On the other hand, the delivery model presents opportunities to make more cost-effective use of resources than at present. These include:

- more extensive use of learner-based methods, such as open learning and discovery learning via resource-based methods;
- staff developing advisory and tutorial roles, rather than teaching and instructing;
- guiding workplace learning;
- developing assessment to supervisors on the job;
- concentrating on delivering specific programmes to meet clearly defined needs.

In order to realise the benefits, a good deal of time and resources need to be invested at the 'front end', but collaborative ventures in establishing models of good practice, such as those currently being undertaken by CITB, the Training Agency and the Further Education Unit among others, will help keep the pursuit of wild geese to a minimum.

The opportunities offered by a system which reduces obstacles to competence will be more attractive to those who find the existing avenues inappropriate for a number of reasons. The disaffection may stem from the content of the programmes (ie much is included in the syllabuses that is irrelevant to an individual's needs) or from the context in which they are delivered (ie work-based learning may enable busy adults to update and develop skills without losing too much pay, and may be seen as much more relevant). In this way, the scope of the market for competence should be increased considerably.

HOW WILL CURRENT PRACTICE CHANGE?

It is always easier to suggest changes in the operation of any set of procedures than actually to implement those changes, and CITB is acutely aware of the implications of NVQs and credit accumulation for those who have to deliver them. Undoubtedly the perceptions of NCVQ itself have changed somewhat since its inception, with definitions and responsibilities becoming more clearly defined.

This will continue as more evidence of implementation and delivery becomes available, and LIBs must assist in accelerating this process by setting up and monitoring as many pilot projects as possible and, most important, by ensuring that the information emerging from these models is disseminated widely. This is clearly a role for the Training Agency and NCVQ itself, and we must hope that both organisations assume a considerably higher profile in this area than they have in the past.

Given the caveats, it is none the less possible to identify clear areas where new or modified practices (in this instance in the context of the construction industry), must be introduced by colleges if they are to survive in the market-place for competence-based programmes.

Diagnosis

Most colleges and training agency approved managing agencies for YTS and ET programmes undertake little diagnosis of learning or training needs at the moment. This may involve trying to ensure as close a match as possible between the trainees' needs and the programmes on offer, and in many instances it is successful as far as it goes. The process falls down however, when the pharmacy from which the educational medicine is prescribed contains only a standard range of pills and potions. Our problem to date, certainly in the construction sector, has been that while the standard prescription has worked wonderfully well for a number of individuals and employers, the majority find our offerings unpalatable or ineffective.

So we must ensure that vocational qualifications begin to reflect the needs of industry rather than the convenience to ourselves as deliverers, and, as has already been outlined, that the concepts of coherence (clearly identifiable paths from Levels I to IV and above) and credit accumulation lead to a much closer fit between needs and offerings. Diagnosis however, will need to be undertaken at two distinct levels, that is, on a company/industry basis, and on an individual basis.

The company dimension

Colleges will need to establish formal links with the local economy. In the construction industry particularly this will mean more than a comfortable regular chat with a group of local firms whose continued support can be relied on. Links must be made with the smaller employers who still find no attraction in long-duration off-the-job courses, and who represent more than 90 per cent of the firms currently operating in the industry.

This is a vast untapped market, and colleges should be setting up mechanisms *now* for getting the message across, and finding out what the precise skill needs of these people are, and what forms of training they will find acceptable. The mix of both content and method will depend on this liaison, and vital information can be gathered which will enable resources to be deployed in a cost-effective way.

Developments such as drop-in workshops, peripatetic tutors, open learning resource banks and 48-week opening will take time to implement. Although NVQs may not be available in great numbers, or at appropriate levels, at the moment, forward-thinking colleges have already realised that these sort of developments are desirable in any case, and their early implementation will ensure that they are well positioned to take full advantage of the emerging system at every stage in its development.

In the construction industry, the company dimension will also embrace the training needs of employers who move into a locality to undertake a contract. These firms may not be local, but for large contracts they may be playing a significant role in the development of the local economy for one, two or three years. What mechanisms are in place to help identify the learning needs of the workforce employed on the site? With credit accumulation becoming a reality remember that people will be 'carrying' credits with them, perhaps accumulated from a college close to their previous site, and may seek or indeed expect to be able to pursue such programmes during their time in your locality.

This market expectation reinforces the point that dynamic and forward-thinking colleges will expand and thrive at the expense of the dilatory. Colleges which cannot or will not meet the needs of a mobile workforce such as that employed in construction operations will find life with NVQs very difficult.

The individual dimension

This last point leads on logically to the need for colleges to offer a diagnostic service to individuals as well as to companies. It will be essential for colleges to offer profiling and counselling facilities to individuals who transfer into their catchment area, and to those who are attracted by the unit-based system and wish to identify the competence they already possess and how they can build on it.

This accreditation of prior learning/achievement is a key area for colleges to address, and will be particularly problematic in the short term before the National Record of Vocational Achievement (NROVA) is fully implemented and trainees themselves are unsure of what is available and how the new system works.

In the construction industry it is unlikely that vast numbers of mature individuals will descend upon colleges and demand that their prior achievements be recognised and an appropriate NVQ be awarded forthwith. There will undoubtedly be some enquiries of this nature, but it is more likely that individuals will be looking towards new 'tailored' qualifications rather than back at what they have done in the past.

There must be a filter, however, which will allow counselling and guidance to be offered as to what routes are most relevant to individual needs. Traditionally consumers of vocational training have been expected to accept a very narrow range of products delivered in a very limited number of ways. The only exceptions to this rule tended to be where open learning had invaded the system, often via the medium of the former MSC's Open Tech programme.

In the construction industry this was exemplified by the site management Open Tech programme, which offered an almost infinite mix of packages to the trainee, drawn from a resource of 200 or so packages. There were mandatory packages, and mandatory modules (which formed a 'core' of key supervisory elements), overlaid by a choice of optional packages, the selection of which was dependent on the nature of each individual's particular working environment.

The open learning centres which did their marketing research and promotion thoroughly, profited from open learning. Those that sat and waited are probably still sitting and waiting.

Flexibility

We have a key here, then, for beginning to organise a competence-based delivery mechanism. Flexibility, based on the three established tenets of open learning – time, pace and place – will provide a model for development:

Time = the choice to start when the student wants.
Pace = each student to progress at his or her own pace.
Place = the choice of where the learning will take place.

Again, it is highly unlikely that providers will be able to deliver a totally flexible system, but where compromises have to be made, they should be made with the knowledge of what local employers and individuals want, so that as few people as possible are 'disenfranchised' by the system. In the construction industry, we have already seen that a majority of the potential market effectively declines the offer to acquire or update skills.

By addressing each of these issues it will be possible to meet the needs of a substantially larger number of people and a larger number again will find that the content of the new competence-based systems are directly relevant to the jobs they are doing, particularly these 'new' groupings of competences we explored under 'What Opportunities?' above. Such a framework will also enable providers to react more quickly to changes in demand. With a 'menu'-driven content, and a delivery system which in part is not linear and unidirectional but can cope with new entrants throughout the year and for varying durations of training, it will be possible to meet the demands of new sites and the influx of new labour (see under 'Diagnosis'), new technologies, new legislation and even new occupations.

All this talk of flexibility will undoubtedly have brought forth howls of outrage from colleges, in particular, who will feel aggrieved that they can do only so much with the syllabuses and training schemes they are given. Others will claim flexibility is their watchword in any case (although evidence suggests otherwise). However, LIBs and Awarding Bodies have key rôles to play in achieving this goal, as it is their function to give a clear lead as regards standards, assessment mechanisms and preferred competence 'groupings' which will lead to industrially-recognised qualifications.

Making new links

This leads to the new channels of communication that now must be established to allow colleges to obtain accurate and current information on the emerging complexion of NVQs. Because of the byzantine nature of the NVQ development model, this will require contact with both LIBs and Awarding Bodies, and it might be worth establishing the terms of reference of each of these before proceeding.

The LIB is charged with establishing employment-led standards of occupational competence for a specified industrial commercial or service sector. It must also ensure that a coherent framework of levels for vocational awards relating to these competences is put in place, and that suitable Awarding Bodies for the qualifications are identified.

It is at this point that the Awarding Body assumes prominence, since it is this organisation (or groups of organisations) that will enter into a contractual relationship with NCVQ. To do so it must satisfy seven specified criteria relating to the award. These are:

1 to have a recognised standing with employers and employees alike;
2 to maintain and monitor the quality and relevance of the award to the occupational group to which it relates;
3 to liaise with NCVQ and others (most notably the Training Agency) involved in developing occupational standards to ensure the further development of the NVQ framework;
4 to have the capability and experience to carry out assessment;
5 to be able to develop and administer a system of credit accumulation, recording and certification;
6 to monitor and apply quality assurance mechanisms regularly;

7 to meet the NCVQ guidelines, which will require reviewing the
   award during the period of accreditation.

Providers then, will need to consider relationships in the development
phase, so that concurrent developments within the organisation, such
as resourcing, marketing, timetabling, staff development and so on
are made in advance of the introduction of new awards; and in the
implementation   phase,   so   that   assessment   requirements,
administrative procedures and so on are appropriate to the new
awards.

The prudent college or managing agent will wish to work alongside
as many of the putative bodies as it can to enable adequate forward
planning to take place. Undoubtedly many LIBs and Awarding
Bodies will develop communication channels and some, such as
CITB, will have done so already. However, it is the responsibility of
each college to develop its own internal competence in handling and
delivering the new system, and many will be shocked by the
responsibility which an output system places on deliverers generally.
While general guidance, preferred models and assessment criteria will
in most cases be made available, means of delivery and times of
attendance and assessment will be locally determined, so it will not be
possible to seek refuge in last year's timetable!

A further element in our college structure is the establishment of a
focus for liaison with as wide a range of industries and Awarding
Bodies as possible and, most important, the dissemination of information to relevant departments with recommendations for action. The
role will essentially be one of co-ordination, but is clearly linked to staff
development issues as well. Such a group will:

- prevent a proliferation of communications between different
  parts of the institution and a whole plethora of external agencies,
  eg Awarding Bodies, LIBs, NCVQ and the Training Agency;
- provide an information base, where expertise gained in discussions with these bodies can be passed on throughout the
  institution;
- ensure that a coherent policy emerges.

The CITB as Lead Industry Body for construction has
implemented a range of mechanisms by which colleges and other
providers can be kept up to date, or can receive basic information on
NVQs in construction which includes videos, leaflets and handbooks
on procedures, and a newsletter *NVQ Recorder* which provides
bulletins on the current state of play.

However, with the development and introduction of any new

system, it is difficult to strike the correct balance between statements of fact, ie what has been achieved, and statements of intent, ie what we aim to achieve. This is particularly difficult when, as we have seen, responsibility for the awards changes hands at the development/ implementation interface and the Awarding Body takes over. Thus the ultimate decisions about assessment, and recording procedures will rest with Awarding Bodies, but much of the groundwork and feasibility studies into the merit of alternative systems will have been undertaken by the Lead Industry Body.

In the context of the construction industry, the CITB has organised and run the training schemes for years, while the certification and conferal of industry recognition has been similarly clearly identified, with City & Guilds or BTEC offering the knowledge element and the National Joint Councils, or joint industry boards, the craft certificate.

It is likely that this composite arrangement will continue, with the industry councils signing a contract with the NCVQ, and CITB offering a range of services, some in conjunction with the certificating bodies, which will broadly ensure that the criteria for Awarding Bodies (the seven elements described earlier) are adequately addressed.

Assessment

Because of the emphasis placed on outcomes, the logical place to assess competence is at the demonstration of that particular task or skill in the workplace, or a simulation thereof. To assess the knowledge and experience required and to ensure that the demonstration of the competence was not successfully achieved by pure chance, some form of contextual questioning will be required and this may be undertaken by verbal questioning, a self assessment paper or a written exercise.

What emerges is a range of assessment opportunities, the precise combination of which will probably be determined by the Awarding Body (in consultation with the LIB), but there will be some latitude for local decisions as to whether, for instance, practical skills will be demonstrated in the college workshop or, where adequate facilities do not exist, on site. It is here, however, that the construction industry presents a unique set of factors which together make the development of a work-based assessment option inordinately difficult.

Consider these issues:

- the variable nature of the building site, where conditions under which tasks undertaken differ from site to site, and also from day to day;
- in an industry where the majority of firms are small, very small

in most cases, who will be responsible for the assessment in these types of organisation?
- the temporary and highly mobile nature of the site.

Quite how standards can be assessed objectively in this type of environment is not yet clear.

However, it should be possible to establish a battery of assessment methods, each of which adhere to the same assessment criteria (this will be achieved by a common assessors' training pack, working through which will be a necessary prerequisite for any would-be assessor), use the same assessment tools (checklists against performance criteria, and a signing off slip on completion to be signed by assessor and trainee) and be moderated regularly by course verifiers who would operate on behalf of the Awarding Body. Assessors may be individuals in companies, or groups of lecturers in colleges. They will be allocated a reference number on successful completion of the training package mentioned above. This 'licence to assess' will be reviewed from time to time in accordance with NCVQ criteria for Awarding Bodies, and the monitoring arrangements will necessarily need to be more regular and more stringent than those often employed at present by Awarding Bodies.

CONCLUSION

In summarising the likely implications for FE, then, we can see that certain key activities have emerged which will together determine the internal organisation required by institutions if the opportunities offered by the NVQ framework are to be grasped. These are:

1 Liaison with local industry, embracing marketing and advisory services. These groups will also need to be working groups involving as many firms as possible, not simply the largest and most compliant.
2 Communication with Awarding Bodies and Lead Industry Bodies: with the former to find out exactly what needs to be done to launch the new programmes; and with the latter to begin to plan for the implementation of the new awards.
3 Both these tasks will require cross-curricular NVQ focus groups, to develop in-house skills and expertise and to spread information via departmental contacts througout the college.
4 Pre-entry guidance and counselling will need to be established in order to assess prior learning, determine the extent to which credits have been accumulated and in what areas (interpreting information from NROVA).

5 The range of delivery mechnisms which can be deployed will have to be reviewed. Workshops, resource-based learning, open learning, in-company courses and so on will all play a part. A unidirectional delivery strategy will be inadequate to meet the demands of the new system.

Figure 5.2 shows the features which will enable colleges to exploit the new construction industry qualifications.

Each college will find its own ways to meet the new demands of delivering NVQs, but it is important that all institutions undertake a thoroughgoing review of the processes they can deploy to identify

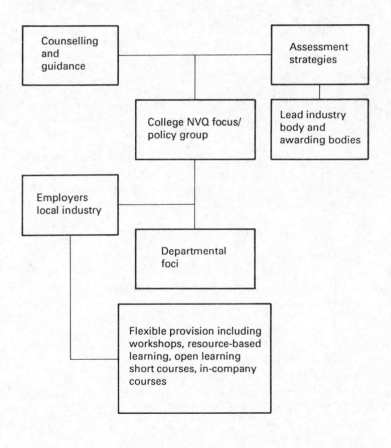

Figure 5.2 *Aspects of college delivery*

trainee and/or employer requirements, deliver the requisite units in a flexible way and assess them, in the workplace if necessary.

These processes should be addressed by all colleges in any case, since they will contribute to an increasingly sensitive and responsive approach to education and training. The message is clearly that provided the mechanisms are in place, then colleges will be able to exploit any future developments emerging from government, industry or commerce.

6. Engineering training and further education: a changing relationship

John Millington

The theme of this chapter is that the relationship between training and education (with particular reference to engineering but relevant elsewhere) has been unclear for many years, and that the effects of this have been both beneficial and harmful. It is too simplistic to disregard, or be contemptuous of, the differences between training and education; to do so ignores the benefits and puts them at risk. Similarly to claim too much for one part or the other of the formation[1] process reinforces divisions in previous processes which had too little integration. The formation of employees and potential employees has often been more controlled by processes than by outcomes and by rules of institutions rather than the interests of the participants.

Despite some major structural faults, not all has been bad in our training and education systems and provision. NCVQ is carefully, but not destructively, creating new structures but is not discarding all that was done before as inappropriate. Indeed if there was not a great deal of established good practice on which to build, the prospects of successfully initiating a new system on the scale now in hand would be poor. The difficulty lies in that there are so many characteristics of vocational qualifications that existing good practice in all of them does not exist in any one previous implementation. All those involved in a highly idiosyncratic range of qualification provisions, developed for different purposes, even including restricting the number of those able to qualify, are therefore finding that cherished traditions are under question.

Engineering training and education is no exception. This contribution will review the good and less good features of the past so that the

---

[1] Formation is a useful term to encompass the idea of a process embracing both training and education which was introduced in the Finniston Report *Engineering Our Future*. It will be used in that sense throughout.

new system can be seen to be building a structure which removes inhibitions to progress while strengthening some desirable characteristics which have been refined over many years. It will also look to new challenges and opportunities in engineering further education.

TRAINING AND EDUCATION: OUTMODED CONCEPTS?

It is easy, and even fashionable, to blame some of the weaknesses of our past systems of vocational preparation and qualifications on separate concepts of training and education, and to question whether the two terms have any distinguishing meaning. Institutionalised divisions arise because different government departments are responsible for policies in education and training. These have led to differences in financial arrangements which often seem arbitrary. NCVQ is however concerned with outcomes rather than processes or institutions and is effectively working across the barriers between education and training in the interests of the competences of all individuals. The benefits of this may be what have been claimed in arguments for a Department of Education and Training. Structural and financial divisions can, I hope, be overcome without losing the intrinsic qualities of either training or education. In working across institutional boundaries the Training Agency and its precursors have influenced education in recent years in ways that would not have been possible for the DES.

Industry, through statutory training organisations such as ITBs and other mechanisms, has set standards for vocational qualifications based on workplace competences. Certain educational attainments have usually been expected before and as part of the vocational qualification. Professional bodies have also set standards for membership reflecting employment competences but also often having an eye to status through exclusivity. The industrial approach has recognised the additive value of education even if it did not correspond to the immediate development of competences. Professional bodies have usually taken educational awards as their starting point and added a more generalised requirement for appropriate experience. Whether education is seen as adding to training or setting 'standards' as a basis for training, both approaches recognise a difference between the components of formation. There are opportunities, and good reasons, for a greater integration of the two elements, but there is a danger that integration brought about from one or other side of the divide may

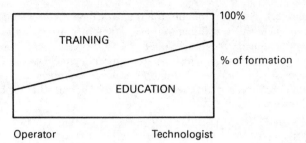

Figure 6.1 *The formation process*

devalue one element to the extent that the formation process is diminished.

There have been artificial divisions within education and within training just as there are between them. It is to NCVQ's credit that these are also being questioned and weakened. In engineering there have been different formation processes for operator, craft, technician and technologist levels. In England and Wales, but not in Scotland where there is an integration proceeding from craft and technician levels, there are different educational awarding bodies. There are even sub-divisions within these levels of occupation. In practice these levels of occupation overlap considerably and vary from person to person, from employer to employer and from time to time. One of the structural difficulties has been that the processes of training and education assumed that there were distinct rôles in industry for which decisions about the formation process had to be made at the outset of a career. Since employers and individuals often did not know what their competence needs would be at the end of a long process there were many mismatches in the actual experience of those involved. It became common for craft trainees to study for technician qualifications for the good of their future rather than for relevance to their training. Many graduates were employed as technicians. The institutional barriers did not permit a mix of educational experiences across the supposed levels. Nevertheless, because the different nature of education and training was recognised, many employers and individuals benefited from the educational experience and many careers grew as a result. Others were disadvantaged by a lack of relevance in their education. By weakening the artificial boundaries in employment levels and encouraging a more flexible approach to formation reflecting individual needs, NCVQ will increase the relevance and utility of further education without restricting participants to a particular process or course of study for several years.

Figure 6.1 illustrates roughly the way in which the proportion of what we have called training and education vary according to the range of engineering occupational rôles described until now as operator, craft, technician, technician engineer and technologist. The educational component of formation is never unimportant and is sometimes more central to the formation process than what we have called training.

It is difficult to conceive of any rôle for which training of more than the most superficial kind is needed which does not require more than the job knowledge for routine tasks. It is in identifying and specifying what is needed for real competence that LIBs have a difficult task. Delivering those requirements will present new challenges for industry and colleges.

COMPETENCE: A NEW SYNTHESIS

That competence implies more than training and more than education, and more than them both together as understood in the past, was stressed by Professor Peter Thompson at an EITB seminar in December 1988. He re-emphasised the essential breadth implied by this concept at the NCVQ annual conference in March 1989. That emphasis is welcomed by those who had feared a narrow, mechanistic interpretation. Competence is the ability to carry out workplace tasks and activities with efficiency, reliability and confidence. Since workplace tasks (except at the most modest levels) are seldom merely repetitive, a mastery beyond mere performance skills is needed for efficiency and reliability and to enable work to be done with the confidence that provides job satisfaction and self motivation. Competence implies an ability to adapt to different circumstances of materials, technology, clients' needs and those other variations which occur in working conditions and which cannot be wholly predicted and pre-programmed. Flexibility, often stressed by employers as among the most valued of attributes in employees, must be built on a confident mastery of known techniques, materials, processes and technology underpinned by a knowledge and understanding of the underlying principles which enable new circumstances to be dealt with confidently. This will be recognised as the traditional function of further and higher education. At its best further and higher education has in fact delivered that understanding but in practice the relationship between the education and the industrial competences it was intended to underpin was often tenuous to the point of being undiscernible.

Just as NCVQ is helping to synthesise the different institutional interests and traditions in its structures, so the concept of competence is a vehicle for synthesising the best qualities of previous training and education provision. It is for those who plan and provide for the formation of people for employment to take the broad approach to interpretations of competence that Professor Thompson and others stress. When vocational competences in other countries are studied it is their breadth and flexibility which are praised. A narrow concept of competence as immediate job skills would diminish what we already have when supposedly skilled people are unable to adapt to change. At its best our vocational preparation has combined both immediate skills and a depth of understanding which enabled people to be flexible. EITB-approved training has always had a broad base with supporting education. Unfortunately not enough of those in employment have had such a vocational preparation. Identifying competences and achieving proper standards in them provides a new opportunity to extend the best practices to all.

TRADITIONAL FE: QUALITIES AND DEFICIENCIES

Further education has served many purposes, and different expectations have caused some strong prejudices for and against it. The Industrial Training Act of 1964 reinforced the separation of training and further education so that training was the responsibility of industry and was not to be provided by colleges except as a contract service at full cost. Some industries, usually with a tradition of training, formalised their arrangements accordingly. In engineering, construction and road transport, for example, employer-financed training with a broad base and specialised continuation was supported by college courses providing the underpinning knowledge and understanding. For some other industries colleges themselves filled the need for training and provided full-time courses of both training and education at no direct cost to employers. Thus employers in industries which did not plan and provide their own training were thereby rewarded and, ironically, colleges which helped them were commended for doing so. Within engineering, where the costs of training were clearly to be borne by employers, some employers, not following EITB guidelines, expected colleges to provide all the training and education for their 'apprentices' in a day each week. Some even looked to colleges for ready trained employees. A personnel director of an off-shore engineering company complained to me once that he wanted 40 trained technicians and could find no college with them waiting for him!

Because FE has generally responded to the demands made by local industry, irrespective of central policies, different practices developed even within the same requirements of examining and validating bodies. That colleges should develop their own approaches to teaching and learning is desirable but within the variety which resulted were some models of excellence by any educational criteria while others failed to meet the aims and had little chance of doing so. Unfortunately bad experiences are given more publicity, if only in conversations among industrial staff, than the best. Many criticisms of certain FE courses reflect a local implementation and not what the course is designed to be. A wholly consistent and objective interpretation of 'standards' is neither possible nor desirable. Progress often follows unplanned initiatives which show what can be achieved. Monitoring of performance against standards should prevent abuses, not inhibit good practice. A review of some past experience may clarify this point and help to avoid poor practice in future. The provision of further education is no longer a closed shop and the distinctive nature and quality of what colleges offer will determine both their reputation and their prosperity.

To illustrate and clarify the dangers of too varied an interpretation of 'education' in further 'education' I shall refer to two national course developments of recent years. Both had national publicity, documentation and regulations but both led to excellent provision in some colleges and very poor provision in others despite the existence of national standards and controls. They make a case for better monitoring in future.

The first of the examples is the C&G Engineering Craft Studies Courses following EITB's training recommendations for craft skills in the early 1970s. These courses made no attempt to develop craft skills (to the dismay of some employers and some colleges) as had their predecessors. Instead they set out the principles which underlie the skills in such a way that the specific skills being acquired in industry were generalised so as to be understood and made applicable to circumstances, materials and technology beyond those encountered during the skill acquisition itself. This meant something quite different from science and mathematics. It provides a practical and developed example of what NCVQ calls 'the underpinning knowledge and understanding'. Regrettably some colleges continued to treat the course as book-based theory and made a classroom course of it with an hour or two of substitute skill training. Enough colleges did recognise the essential nature of the courses to show that so-called non-academic young people could enjoy a genuinely educational course which was both demanding and stimulating.

This was because the Craft Studies Courses were based on active learning in practical contexts; not practical workshop techniques but investigations, assignments and projects which developed the understanding of the principles supporting the craft skills. An example may be necessary to illustrate the point. A trainee turner would learn to turn skilfully; this involves more than the manual skill alone. It requires learning to plan a sequence of operations; to select appropriate tools and to secure them properly; to hold the work-piece appropriately, to select the right spindle and cutting speeds; to select suitable lubricants; to measure and control the results to the required accuracy. All that requires planned training over a long time with many different opportunities to practice. It also requires the acquisition of a considerable amount of knowledge on the way. What would be wrong during the training process would be for the instructor to spend time showing wrong techniques or for the trainee to try these out; similarly it would be a distraction without much chance of leading to retention to spend time on possibilities not available there and then.

During the separate Craft Studies courses things were different. The scheme for Mechanical Engineering made no mention of turning or other specific machining process. What it did was to cover the principles of all machining procesesses by dealing with work-holding, tool-holding, material removal, dimensional control and planning (all with health and safety in mind). The student at college would carry out guided investigations into the different ways of work-holding, tool-holding, cutting and so on, taking known techniques to their limits and beyond to develop an understanding of the principles. The effect of progressively different tool cutting angles and materials, or of cutting speeds, or of lubricants was discovered by systematic investigation, taking each to the point at which the results were unacceptable. Such activities would have been a distraction for both instructors and trainees during training but were recognised as serving a different purpose at college. The demands which could be made of supposedly non-academic students when acquiring an understanding of these complex relationships in a practical context rather than mainly from verbal sources was a revelation to many teachers and enormously satisfying for the young people concerned. It is in the nature of activity-based learning that different abilities and backgrounds can be provided for in ways that classroom learning cannot easily emulate.

If this represented some of the best in further education the same Craft Studies Courses illustrate some of the worst. There were colleges which ignored the aims of the courses and used timetables, resources and teaching approaches virtually identical to the superseded courses.

By providing examination preparation by classroom talk and chalk (some happily talked of lecturing to craft trainees!) and interpreting the practical requirements as being skill training (as if two hours a week could provide that) these colleges came to dislike the Craft Studies Courses as being too academic, the students complained that the courses were boring and too much like school, and employers saw little benefit either in understanding and motivation or in enhanced ability. Many employers, having selected craft trainees according to EITB recommendations, considered TEC and later BTEC courses to be more demanding and stimulating for their craft trainees. This was often encouraged by colleges which regarded the courses as different only in academic level rather than in kind and relevance. This academic drift led to some trainees becoming motivated to acquire technician FE awards and to enhance their employment prospects. Some employers were also happy to use the academic courses as selection instruments for transfer and promotion purposes. However, for employers there was a disruption in the planned supply of competent craftsmen. For many students the more academic nature of the technician courses failed to provide that understanding of craft principles which would have led to mastery levels of competence and left them with a perception of FE as merely book learning at which they had not done well. Additionally the staff of colleges were able to achieve less in courses designed for technician trainees when many students were receiving craft training and there was often dissatisfaction with standards achieved in those courses as a result.

All this was with the well-intentioned desire to give young people the opportunity to do as well as they could. In fact by pressing students into the highest academic level of course in which they might survive colleges, and consenting employers, achieved the opposite of their intentions in most cases. Instead of achieving mastery levels of competence, with all the self-confidence and motivation that gives, the young people scraped by (if they were successful at all) in a more academic course which merely acted as a hurdle. The Peter Principle applies in education as much as in employment.

The worst characteristics of further education can be further illustrated through the same Craft Studies Courses when they were used for young people not in employment at all. As employment opportunities for young people decreased many colleges developed full-time courses for those interested in engineering at craft level. These courses led to Craft Studies certificates at Part I level and provided some practical training in place of what would have been obtained in industry. However, in some cases the courses covered the work not merely for one Craft Studies Course (which would have been the case for employed trainees being trained in industry for four days a week) but for several. The extra Craft Studies Courses should have needed extra practical training for each skill area covered; instead, the time taken by the extra FE studies meant decreasing time for the practical competences the young people wished to acquire to give them the confidence to seek employment. The belief in the value of academic achievements over industrial competences had deprived young people of a genuinely educational experience in favour of certificate collecting. Both the young people and subsequent employers who assumed that the FE certificates (without the training they had been designed to supplement) were themselves guarantees of competence were sadly disillusioned.

The second illustration is at technician level. When TEC introduced its new awards it emphasised that all programmes were to develop a range of personal and transferable skills as part of the process of learning the content of the units. Units stressed that they did not constitute a teaching scheme and that the objectives could be achieved through a variety of activity methods. Many colleges took advantage of this to provide genuinely educational experiences which contributed to technician level competences while the students were acquiring the knowledge and understanding appropriate to their training. Regrettably some other colleges were overcome by what they saw as a heavy load of book learning and abandoned active learning (well established in the preceding Joint Committee schemes) and any attempt to develop transferable skills. Because of the lack of motivation of students for this approach attainments declined and even more formal teaching was used to try to enable students to reach the expected standards of knowledge retention. Eventually BTEC (after BEC and TEC merged) revised its requirements so that active learning methods through assignments of various kinds was obligatory. It also changed the entry requirements so that colleges were not able to admit students to national level courses with inadequate preparation, thereby reducing the academic pressures on many entrants.

These comparisons of the excellence of the best provision of engineering further education and the worst, often with good intentions, are a necessary warning. We must learn from them if we are to ensure that the new system of vocational qualifications, based on the broad concept of competence, builds on past successes. Academic approaches that do not lead to increased competences must not be perpetuated, as old practices often have been after previous reforms in further education.

THE IMPORTANCE OF UNDERPINNING KNOWLEDGE AND UNDERSTANDING

Before NCVQ made it necessary to do so EITB was already working to disaggregate the content of its training recommendations, so that the discontinuities between craft, technician and technician engineer training were removed and credit accumulation could be implemented. Those not receiving planned training leading to complete certification would benefit immediately from credit accumulation, and others wishing to add to initial qualifications, or to change direction at any time, would find that starting a new programme from scratch was no longer necessary. This work within EITB, known as the *Coherence Project*, was given more importance by NCVQ because it was consistent with the requirement for LIBs to lay down specifications of competence. This made it possible for elements and units to be defined individually and their performance criteria to be stated independently of other units or elements, and also independently of the process by which the competences are acquired. NCVQ has discarded the traditional emphasis on entry requirements, and on complete courses of training and/or further education planned from the outset for large categories of people and has established a system based on individual programmes for the needs of individual trainees and employers (but with the protection of national *employment standards* to avoid narrowness). The training standards specified by LIBs such as EITB provide a starting point for a new approach in which the former training and educational components of formation can be integrated despite the disaggregation of the requirements into units and elements.

Disaggregation presents major operational problems for further education. EITB is working effectively on the training problems. In the case of the 'educational' components the problems are greater and there is certainly a risk of losing more than is gained. The underpinning knowledge and understanding required for competences can be classified in three groups:

1 The immediate knowledge and understanding needed for each unit or element of competence; the 'know how' which is the stock in trade of a competent person.
2 The knowledge and understanding needed to cope with developments in the technology or with applications of the competence in unfamiliar contexts; the underlying principles or 'know why' on which mastery depends.
3 The integrating personal and generic competences which apply across many vocational activities; the 'will do' commitment to

the quality of work and to the employer's and client's (and the community's) interests.

While the first group can, to advantage, be dealt with in an integrated way as the elements and units of competence are being acquired, the other two groups are not readily, or even at all, developed in disaggregated parts. They require a more progressive development in a wide variety of contexts and the opportunity to reflect and grow. They require learning contexts separate from those in which skills are initially acquired. Skill acquisition demands care, precision, immediate feedback and practice without distraction.

Clearly not all employment requires these three groups of underpinning knowledge and understanding to the same degree although any that requires some planned training is unlikely not to need some measure of all three. For the most modest jobs the fact of competent performance may itself subsume the necessary knowledge and understanding and group 1 predominates. For more demanding jobs, even though essentially practical, the knowledge and understanding needed to cope with all situations flexibly cannot be developed or observed in a limited number of applications; it might take a year for a skilled craftsman or -woman to acquire and demonstrate the knowledge and understanding which gives the self-confidence of genuine competence. For jobs in which a great deal of discretion and decision-making is involved, the ability to discriminate among a range of possibilities and to generalise from previous experiences to the new one depends on the second level of underpinning knowledge and understanding to a high degree, and single demonstrations cannot show that it has been acquired.

It is in the planned and effective delivery of the second and, in a contributory way, third groups of underpinning knowledge and understanding that engineering FE can provide a distinctive and (if the best of past practices are taken as the starting point) a distinguished place in the competence-based system. This does not mean that FE colleges have no place in the delivery of the main competences together with the integrated 'know how'. In this respect FE can offer its services on a fee basis to industry: colleges can also make provision in a variety of courses as it has in the past and be subject to LIB monitoring of standards if NVQ or NROVA recognition is required. Nor does it mean that only FE colleges will be able to provide for the delivery of the 'know why' and 'will do' categories of underpinning knowledge and understanding as has been nearly (but not entirely) the case in the past. If employers, or others on their behalf, can enable people to acquire these competences, again subject to LIB monitoring of standards achieved, then NCVQ will not protect any supposed vested rights. FE can deliver the 'know why' and at least the basis of the 'will do' groups of underpinning knowledge and understanding with a quality which others will have difficulty in matching. The fact that FE has never charged full costs to students and employers for this education, may give colleges the edge over commercial competition, given that they have the resources to continue with such a strategy.

It is important that FE retains its market by the quality of its provision. Just as the NCVQ and EITB concept of underpinning knowledge and understanding is not a trivial component of competence, so its provision in the new climate will not be a trivial matter for colleges.

FE AWARDS: A NEW REALISM

Those who have regarded the awards of FE validating and certificating bodies as complete vocational qualifications will face a new realism about the status of such awards. This will not be hard for those others who have had a clear concept of the distinctive nature of engineering further education as one component of the formation process and who have ensured that the experiences of participants, and the competences they acquire, were different from, but complementary to, those acquired in industrial training. Whether that training took place in industry, or in colleges on a contract basis, or in some alternative arrangement under YTS, or full-time course provision, does not alter the argument. The different nature and qualities of FE awards is recognised by many employers who place considerable reliance on them. This is partly because the certification by EITB reflects standards demonstrated in the employer's own workplace (as well as in the FE) and the recognition by EITB confirms what is already known. The FE award adds an extra dimension in acheivements of trainees to those gained in the company. In this the FE award has a respect and status which goes beyond its direct utilitarian value. This needs to be protected.

The confusion about the nature and rôle of FE awards (I am intentionally avoiding the term *qualifications* since FE awards are potentially contributory components of NVQs, as they have always been for the EITB) stems from the institutional confusion described earlier. NCVQ, in working across the boundaries of government departments and of the training-education institutions, is forcing a new realism about the nature of FE courses and awards. If, as some in FE as well as elsewhere, have claimed there is no difference between training and further education then the rationale for FE is weakened and may be destroyed. If there was such an equation then the need for those undertaking planned training to EITB craft or technician standards to attend college for day-release FE would be undermined. After all, the training of craft and technician trainees in industry occupies over 80 per cent of the trainee's time; since it is clear that FE courses have provided something additional to any training programme in, for example the development of mathematics and some scientific knowledge together with communication studies (as well as the specialist principles) it is absurd to believe that there could be an approach to the standards of competence developed in industrial training. Even when full-time courses in colleges included some practical work (not the same as practical laboratory and similar work for FE purposes) to substitute for industrial training the amount was far less than would have been provided in industry. In fact many colleges preferred to add more educational elements by way of extra BTEC units or extra C&G specialisms rather than to provide more than a token amount of industrial training. Despite the gross imbalance in time between engineering training and further education, colleges have sometimes claimed to be producing trained technicians or craftsmen in such full time courses. At best only the first stages of EITB's requirements had been achieved and it remained for companies to provide the bulk of the training needed.

Colleges must maintain their best traditions of providing something which is distinctive and which complements training in the new synthesis which NCVQ is creating. Fortunately many can justify the place of FE by their proven performance and not merely as a form of words. Success in FE awards *alone* is neither necessary nor sufficient for either NCVQ's or EITB's concept of employment competences and qualifications. EITB's blanket requirement for FE to be part of the formation process has been a convenient arrangement, but colleges must develop a new realism about the qualities and limitations of FE awards in the new system of vocational qualifications. In doing so they will have the opportunity to enhance the real value of FE as something distinctive and distinguished.

FLEXIBLE PROVISION OF UNDERPINNING KNOWLEDGE AND UNDERSTANDING

Employers have sent their trainees to FE colleges for a number of reasons, some of which may change in the new system. EITB, believing in the value of FE, has required employers to do this for most young trainees, and both finance (through the levy-grant system) and certification (by EITB) depended on the provision of FE. Many employers had used FE colleges for better reasons before EITB appeared. But some employers who provided training to EITB standards have not looked to colleges. Since the 'know how' was being acquired in training there was no great concern about the immediate relevance of FE to that training. FE courses were, however, clearly valued in several ways by other employers: the provision of underpinning knowledge and understanding to enable competences to be applied in new circumstances, the development of each trainee's potential for enhanced rôles in the company (and the industry more generally), and the provision of a basis for progression to subsequent training and FE. The value that some employers placed on FE is illustrated by the fact that, because of the colleges' need to form viable class groups, many employees were placed in FE courses not designed for their training specialism. If direct relevance and utility were the only reason for FE this would not have happened (and it may not be acceptable for NVQ purposes). Many of those responsible for company training had themselves benefited from this multi-level nature of FE and wanted trainees to benefit similarly.

So what is the place of engineering FE courses and awards in the new system? There are two extreme positions which can be anticipated and a range of possibilities in between. It is worth looking at the extremes so as to recognise the boundaries of what faces colleges in the new system.

When EITB, as an LIB, has identified the competences and set standards with criteria of performance for industrial rôles, it will also have specified the relevant underpinning knowledge and understanding in individual units of competence. Some existing or revised FE courses (or units, parts of units or modules within courses) may well be identified as covering the underpinning knowledge and understanding for individual units or complete NVQs. The FE validating or certifying body's certificates will then be accepted by EITB as proving the achievement of the standards by an applicant for an NVQ. NCVQ has recognised the multi-level purposes of traditional FE but has stated that, while the preparation for future courses or for later rôles in industry is valuable for companies and individuals, success in those parts of a course designed for such progression cannot be a requirement for the award of an NVQ or for contributory units. For example, an NVQ corresponding to what has been called technician level must not be refused because a BTEC national level award, previously required by EITB as the FE component of its technician certificate, has not been gained. This is because BTEC national level courses contain material which is designed to prepare students for progression to technician engineer levels of award. For an NVQ corresponding to what has been called craft level similar considerations apply; the C&G awards at Part II level have less content looking beyond this level and so have a closer relationship to the craft training requirements. But EITB has also accepted BTEC awards as the FE component of its craft certificates to recognise the desire of many companies to develop employees' potential to the full and provide a basis for possible retraining as technicians. However well intentioned, success in FE courses designed for technician level trainees clearly cannot be made a requirement for the award of an NVQ which recognises craft competences.

Immediately we see an anomaly caused by the institutional separation of FE awards between C&G, BTEC and CNAA (and other bodies for specialisms other than engineering) when there are no such hard separations between the rôles and needs of the employees in industry. EITB's coherence project is developing a single system to cover all levels from operator to higher technician. It is difficult to see an easy match for this in the FE courses leading to the awards of different bodies with wholly different course structures. The SCOT-VEC provision of FE makes such a match far more easy to conceive; in Scotland there has been a coherent approach to the pattern of FE provision which corresponds well to EITB's new approach, with no hard boundaries between operator, craft and technician levels. The current moves in Scotland to embrace higher technician levels take this process forward in a helpful way.

The two extreme positions can now be seen fairly clearly. At one extreme an employer or trainee may wish for a complete FE course to accompany training in industry as in the past. If the FE courses do in fact contain the material identified as necessary, the FE award can clearly be accepted as meeting the requirements of the LIB. At the other extreme an employer may take advantage of the withdrawal of the levy-grant system in 1991 and see no financial advantage in training employees to national standards and sending them to college for FE at all. This was the situation which the ITBs were created to change, and they certainly did so in engineering, for which the quantity and quality of training and further education increased dramatically after 1964. Through all the vicissitudes of the economy and pressures on training, colleges have consistently had more day-release students (a measure of industrial commitment to training and FE far more positive than the number of full-time students for obvious reasons) in engineering than in any other specialism. The success of EITB in achieving the aims of the 1964 Industrial Training Act was the direct cause of that growth of engineering further education.

It is to be hoped that the removal of the statutory powers of EITB following the White Paper *Employment in the 1990s* will not lead to many employers withdrawing from national standards of training. Indeed if the new Training and Enterprise Councils (TECs) prove effective and the status of NVQs becomes well established much may be built on the record of the past in engineering. So the worst extreme position postulated may not be common. However some employers or applicants may want only the minimum necessary underpinning knowledge and understanding specified by the LIB for a particular NVQ. (This should of course be more than merely the 'know how' previously described, so this does not imply a very narrow interpretation.) The problem then will be to provide a disaggregated FE course to enable the appropriate criteria of performance to be met without requiring the material for progression to be covered also. This may present real problems for colleges and it will tax their ability to provide individual learning opportunities in flexible ways.

Yet another requirement for colleges will be to recognise the achievement of those who, while they may be following complete FE courses, do not gain a whole award but who have demonstrated competence in all or parts of the underpinning knowledge and understanding required for an NVQ or contributory units. Records of achievement for parts of FE courses have not been part of the tradition of colleges, and it requires considerable revision of the structure of courses, of teaching and learning approaches and of assessment techniques, not to say record keeping, to provide for the different outcomes of FE courses now that they cannot be regarded as all-or-nothing products. The modularisation of some FE courses (BTEC courses have always been so designed) does enable single units to be assessed and certificated but even more disaggregation will become necessary. As an obvious example the mathematics required to contribute to the competence of an engineering technician may be found in parts of BTEC units at levels I, II and III but does not require all of those units. Furthermore the requirements for different kinds of technician will not be the same.

All this presents real problems for EITB as an LIB since NCVQ will not allow it to make a blanket requirement for applicants for an NVQ to have a complete FE award as it has done in the past. It also presents problems for the FE validating and certificating bodies in revising the content, presentation, assessment and certification of their courses. It presents real problems for colleges in providing for a wide range of different employer and individual needs.

Just as part certification will become necessary at least for some individual needs, so it will become necessary to give credit for prior achievements. The FE system has always been ready to give individual students access to courses according to evidence of earlier achievements; the phrase 'at the college's discretion', or something like it, has often appeared in course rules when referring to entry requirements. However this openness will become a matter of *duty* for the college and of *right* for the applicant rather than a matter of discretion. Credit for whole years will be too coarse a provision. Colleges have varied in their approach to allowing credit for prior learning even when operating under the same rules. For example the BTEC unit-credit system was intended to provide for some entrants to be exempted from individual units. Some colleges did this because they arranged their timetables and curricular structures to allow individual programme-building; others made little attempt to do so and continued to provide what were in effect grouped courses taken by all students who could not be given exemption for a complete year.

So although there is some experience of giving credit for prior learning the techniques for doing so will have to be refined to provide for the identification, assessment and recording of unit credits. There will be a need for new assessment instruments and an organisation to enable them to be used on demand; both of which will have to be of a kind more systematic and planned and yet more flexible and responsive than has been common in the past.

If the assessment and accreditation of prior learning will require a development of existing techniques the assessment of the learning in the colleges will present new problems, although again some colleges will be more prepared by their past than others. It is a tenet of NCVQ's approach that competence can only be assessed by being observed in performance. Further, the performance should be in actual workplace contexts and only when that is not possible should a simulated workplace context be used. Sitting in an examination room recalling information and solving paper problems carefully constructed to avoid extraneous information and to be solvable in 20 minutes, or selecting from presented options in multi-choice papers, is far from demonstrating competence in workplace contexts. These processes have value in formative and developmental learning as feedback processes but it is the *application* of the underpinning knowledge and understanding which NVQs recognise. While educational institutions of all kinds have always claimed to develop understanding rather than to impart mere information, ways of demonstrating understanding have not often been found. This is not to belittle the need for information and knowledge of facts and principles as tools on which understanding depends; they are necessary but not sufficient. Only by the application of what has been learned in unfamiliar situations can understanding be demonstrated, observed and assessed. This is a challenge to many previous practices in further education. Application in a sense which relates to competence in workplace contexts will require the understanding to examine a task, to discriminate from the information available what is relevant and to select the appropriate knowledge and techniques to provide a solution. The principle that examination questions should give all the information necessary and no more removes the need for such application competences. As a result examination questions have often become more and more narrow and difficult (according to the level of the course) in demanding specific recall of facts, principles and techniques without approaching the level of *competence in application* that is needed in real workplace contexts.

The alternative is to start with the kinds of workplace problems actually met by craftsmen, technicians and others and develop tasks which require information and demand outcomes of less stereotyped sorts. Such tasks need a level of mastery of an inventory of knowledge and techniques which enable the competent person to use them appropriately in the context; to select what is relevant from the information available, to seek necessary information which is not provided and to synthesise the acquired knowledge and understanding with the information specific to the new context in a competent performance.

Some FE staff may feel that such tasks are beyond the ability of most in their courses. Many examples in primary and secondary education and in non-traditional FE suggest this is not so. Programmes such as the now defunct Unified Vocational Preparation (UVP), multi-skilled activities in some MSC and Training Agency schemes have pleasantly surprised many FE staff when they were freed from overloaded academic syllabuses and could develop genuinely educational activities, making demands on young people that were motivating and attainable. There were other colleges which tried to make such people fit into the regime of traditional courses with knowledge acquisition and examinations; not surprisingly they *proved* that the participants weren't up to scratch.

A mistake repeatedly made is to assume that one must acquire knowledge and understanding before it can be applied. In practice knowledge and understanding are most readily acquired through applications when the need to know and understand, and therefore the motivation to learn, is obvious. If learning is designed to take place in a series of tasks based on applications there are a number of beneficial consequences. The ability to apply knowledge is developed progressively without special effort; it is what the process is for. The knowledge needed can be classified in a range from essential to occasionally useful and the emphasis put on it in the learning process can be decided by utility rather than by academic difficulty. The knowledge which is needed at mastery level, and which must therefore be thoroughly learned and practised, can be distinguished from that which needs to be available occasionally and therefore can be resourced from an external source when needed. An almost inevitable outcome will be that much of what has been regarded as essential in FE courses (and yet assessed as satisfactory if only 40 per cent is achieved in assessments!) is there because it is teachable and examinable and because of some notion that 'standards' are at risk if courses are not full of book learning. What NCVQ is requiring of LIBs such as EITB is that NVQs will not require unnecessary knowledge but will ensure that what is necessary is understood to the level of being applied with confidence and mastery in competent performances.

This implies no lowering of standards. It requires the development of real understanding with transferable skills of problem solving, decision making, discrimination and generalisation (among others) which are the distinguishing characteristics of an educated person at any level of competence. The reliance on paper tests for engineering, which is an integrating and synthesising activity at all levels, is itself an abrogation of relevant standards. There have been healthy moves away from such a reliance in recent years but the balance is still to an unnecessarily academic weighting in engineering education in the interests of a supposed rigour or sorting-out procedure. As a consequence engineering has the reputation of being a difficult discipline. Many look for easier options and the sorting-out process discards many potentially valuable contributors to the industry. NCVQ, in looking for clear statements of relevant competence and for demonstrable evidence of those competences, is setting more difficult tasks for trainers and educators since actual engineering tasks are more complex than paper problems. The standards will be higher than before in what matters, the ability to perform real tasks with mastery and understanding, with confidence and quality. That will satisfy both employers and trainees and, in doing so, will give a new level of satisfaction to colleges themselves.

PROVISION OF WHOLE COMPETENCES

Because of the way in which EITB, not alone among ITBs, established a national pattern of training which recognised the distinctive place of further education as complementary to training, it has been open to engineering departments in colleges to provide further education and training on different financial bases. Industry has been statutorily responsible for training and it was therefore clear that any training provided in colleges should be paid for by employers at commercial rates. Some other industries with less planned training found colleges stepping into the breach and providing what were largely training courses at public expense so that employers were able to recruit well-prepared and qualified young people at 17+ and 18+ having contributed nothing directly to their training. The engineering industry, having taken its legal responsibility for training more seriously, paid for such training from the outset and was in effect penalised for doing so. The effect is that engineering departments in colleges are familiar with providing industrial training for employers at commercial rates and under industrial conditions. Training for first year craft and technician trainees occupied up to 46 weeks and (with the FE component) some 38 hours per week. The training was subject to monitoring by both the employer and EITB and both the processes and the standards of performance were set by industry, through EITB, and not by educational bodies or by the colleges themselves.

This means that many engineering departments have a long experience of providing for industry, beyond their educational rôle, and of meeting commercial client-provider demands. The first year EITB training programmes were national in kind, but even with national standards there was always scope for individual employer's special needs to be met, and there were usually alternative providers available to employers if satisfaction was not received. In recent years virtually all colleges have recognised that there is a market in industry and that unless they are in that market their development will be limited. The new system being introduced by NCVQ, coupled with the effects of the education Reform Act and *Employment in the 1990s*, provides new opportunities for engineering departments to market themselves. Again some will no doubt take these opportunities more readily than others.

Some opportunities to meet employer needs in more flexible ways in respect of the underpinning knowledge and understanding have been referred to in the previous section. Provision of that kind will presumably be charged at normal FE rates for educational courses unless special arrangements have to be made for individual employers in what would otherwise be unviable groups. That is merely a development of colleges' normal provision. It is in the competitive field of training that both the NCVQ system and the effects of *Employment in the 1990s* present opportunities for growth in the provision of training and related services for employers at commercial rates.

The disaggregation of training recommendations following the outcomes of EITB's *Coherence Project* will make the previous programmes for first year training less marketable as complete packages. Some employers will continue to want such packages but they will have to be presented in identifiable units of competence which are documented and assessed. The underpinning knowledge and understanding can be integrated, at least to some extent, or partly covered by FE courses which have been identified as fulfilling these requirements. Some employers, including previous users of college training courses, but also including others whose needs have been for more limited training, may well want specified units of competence to be covered by their employees but not a full year off-the-job commitment. The nature of practical training, requiring individual instruction and practice, makes the flexible provision of such units fairly easy. The scope for annual planning and timetabling of the demands on staff and resources will, however, be reduced in the need to respond to shorter term contracts.

So far what has been described is a natural progression for many engineering departments in colleges. It will, however, require new arrangements for providing training in smaller units, for assessing competences and for recording achievements. It will, of course, also require new marketing efforts if former clients are to be retained and new ones found.

An entrepreneurial rôle

There are other, newer, opportunities which will call for new entrepreneurial efforts. The new Training and Enterprise Councils (TECs) will be concerned with the planning of training in their areas and for commissioning provision where it is needed. In engineering there is a great deal of actual or potential provision in companies, group training associations and other locations as well as in colleges. Unlike colleges most other providers of engineering training have not had long lead times of planning and obtaining new resources or of timetabling existing staff and facilities; they have lived by response to client needs. It will be for colleges to convince the TECs as well as individual employers that they can deliver training and its related services competently and flexibly. Again *competently* means, for colleges as much as for trainees, with mastery of known techniques ('know how'), the understanding to work in new contexts ('know why') and the motivation to deliver a quality product ('will do').

The TECs will be responsible for identifying training needs and for ensuring that provision is made to meet those needs; they will not be responsible for setting standards. That remains a national responsibility of LIBs carrying out the functions in standard-setting and monitoring. EITB will cease to exist as a statutory training organisation in 1991 but its successor body is being formed in consultation with the industry and will presumably be both a non-statutory training organisation (NSTO) and an LIB for manufacturing engineering. The LIB defines competences without defining processes; The NSTO will advise (on a commercial basis) on the best processes through codes of practice and other material. The outcomes of EITB's coherence project in units of competence and NVQs will presumably be the basis of the TECs' requirements for standards and certification in the engineering training they plan or commission. Colleges which are already providing for trainees to reach the standards and administrative requirements of these units will be well placed to offer them, and elements within them, to TECs as validated contributions to the provision.

There will be training-related services of new kinds open to colleges which operate in the industrial training field. As NVQs, or units towards them, become the required evidence that standards of competence have been reached, employers and TECs will expect the characteristics associated with NVQs to be in place.

They will expect a service of assessment of prior learning so that all trainees do not have to follow a common programme. They will expect training and assessment to be in actual workplace contexts or such good simulations that there is confidence in the outcomes. They will expect the provider to be recognised by the NSTO as competent so that national standards can be assured.

Each of these expectations can be met by colleges which already have EITB recognition provided that they develop their current provision in the ways indicated. However there may be new financial arrangements involved. In the past EITB has given recognition to colleges which met its standards of staff and resources for training, it has provided training advice, materials and documentation at little or no cost, has monitored standards and has issued certificates. The cost to colleges has been negligible because EITB was supported by the levy system. After 1991 the successor body to EITB will be wholly commercial and its services and materials will have to be paid for accordingly. How this will be arranged is yet to be decided but colleges must expect to pay for NSTO recognition and services just as they charge for their services to employers.

What else may colleges do as entrepreneurs in the new system? One effect of NCVQ's success, and the effect of intra-European work opportunities, might well be that existing employees without formal vocational qualifications will want to accumulate units towards NVQs. Many people in the past received industrial training less than that required by EITB and may have not completed the required FE courses. When these people know that they can be assessed and given credit for elements or units in which they can prove competence rather than having to start courses from scratch, many may wish to take advantage. Colleges, among others, could provide a battery of tests in the actual workplace or in workplace simulations to supplement any other evidence available and record the achievements. The LIB successor to EITB will monitor such records if they are to count towards its NVQs. Perhaps NVQ status will give a new impetus to employer, employee and union interest in having formal recognition of workplace competences as part of the growing trend towards planned human resource development. Colleges could develop a suite of advisory, counselling and assessment services to meet these new interests.

There are also individuals not currently employed in engineering who might with to benefit from such services as a way into the industry. Many competences, or at least elements within them, have common features in different employment fields and their identification can make the subsequent learning period far more effective than if complete programmes have to be followed. The advantage of a system of advisory, counselling and assessment services is that it is inherently flexible, being directed to individual needs; it can therefore be available to clients with many backgrounds and needs provided that the staff involved are fully up to date in their knowledge of what is possible and achievable.

Colleges will, of course, continue to provide for full-time students who, for a variety of reasons, are not in employment or a government-financed training scheme. This group of clients is virtually a captive one since no other institutions can provide such courses of both training and further education at such little direct cost to the young people or their parents. Such provision has been both a success, in that many young people have found in themselves abilities not previously recognised and have been motivated to develop those abilities, and a failure, in that some provision had an over-emphasis on examination preparation with little feel for the activities of engineering. Colleges will continue to provide academic courses and some young people, usually looking for a route into higher education, will benefit from them. Such courses, with their limited practical training, will be unlikely to lead to the acquisition of competences sufficient for the award of an NVQ, although some units may be covered. If colleges want employers to look at the products of their full-time courses as competent at a recognised level they will have to show that NVQ standards have been reached.

The belief that students should be *given the opportunity* to try the *highest* academic level course in which they might succeed has to be questioned. Over-academic provision leads to discontent among students and staff and the inevitable borderline performance of most students. Wastage and failure are endemic; wastage is not merely in those who leave or fail; it is among those who succeed but achieve far less mastery and self-confidence than they would have done in a more suitable course. If they wish to play a full part in a competence-based system colleges must find relevant provision for full-time students as for others. The provision must relate to individual motivation which will be fed by the achievement of recognised competences rather than by achieving a series of near 40 per cent assessments in paper tests which prove little of lasting worth and provide no self-confidence for the future. Further education should not be a series of hurdles which one scrapes over until failure comes. It should be the achievement of worthwhile competence targets to standards which prove a mastery in performance, with an understanding of principles which give the competent person confidence to face new contexts.

At graduate level it is possible for practical competences to be built on a foundation of knowledge and principles. At technician and craft levels the underpinning knowledge and understanding must have something to underpin; it must have demonstrable applications in known and new contexts to prove that understanding has been acquired. Vocational competence is at the heart of the new qualifications and that means *knowing how, knowing why* and *actually doing. Knowing about* the theory and practice, which is what the more academic courses in colleges were reduced to, is not sufficient.

SUMMARY: NEW CHALLENGES AND NEW OPPORTUNITIES

Writing about the new system of vocational qualifications from a viewpoint in EITB it is not possible to be categorical about how colleges of further education will be affected or how they should prepare for and respond to the new challenges. The NVQs so far approved for engineering are based on previous training recommendations, with a strengthening of FE requirements, but they are now being replaced by new schemes. The statutory status of EITB is to end in 1991 and its successor body will have a role as NSTO which is complementary to, but not co-terminous with, its role as LIB. This chapter cannot therefore give the kind of operational and administrative guidance which colleges will need for their detailed work within the new system.

A review of the best qualities of engineering FE of recent years has shown that there is much of value on which to build. At the same time there have been deficiencies in past performance which the new emphasis on competence as the outcome of formation will expose if they are not removed. Colleges have already changed in their approach to entrepreneurial activities and the effect of the Education Reform Act is to give those activities a new impetus. The changes resulting from the introduction of NVQs and from *Employment in the 1990s* make the new freedom of the colleges timely. This chapter has considered some of the ways that colleges will be affected and how they might respond.

What is important is that colleges should not wait for definitive details of what is required of them. Changes will be introduced and opportunities will emerge over a period and will never come to an end. Most of the opportunities will depend on colleges having an inventory of competences of their own to apply to the new circumstances as they arise. The time is already here and partly gone for colleges to develop competences in assessment of prior learning, in workplace assessment of competences, in flexible programme building for a variety of clients far wider than young trainees, in providing records of achievement for less than whole courses, and other techniques. There are already publications of NCVQ, FESC, FEU, the Training Agency and others on these topics. Existing provision presents opportunities to develop the competences before they become essential. That is the function of training and it applies to college staff as much as to their clients. Colleges' own competences, like those of their clients, need to be underpinned with 'know how', 'know why' and 'will do' qualities so that they can work with mastery and self-confidence.

In meeting the new challenges colleges should be conscious and proud of the distinctive contribution that further education, at its best, has made, and can continue to make, to the formation of those who work in a range of engineering occupations. That distinction should be sustained despite the loss of a protected status for whole courses of FE. For many in senior positions in the industry and elsewhere, engineering FE has been the key to careers of great value to themselves, their employers and the country. EITB, its successor body, NCVQ, the TECs and training and education providers all have something to live up to and enhance, as well as deficiencies to remove while developing a new system of vocational qualifications.

Part 3:
Implementing flexible delivery

7. NVQs and the role of guidance in competence-led curricula

Aidan Pettit, Geoff Crook and Ruth Silver

INTRODUCTION

'Guidance' was developed as a concept in education as long ago as 1955 by Ben Morris.[1] He identified; four components of guidance: a diagnosis or 'checking out'; advice; information based on knowledge; and training based on graded skill. Some thought that this definition suggested too directive a form of help and so began to use the term 'counselling'. More recently, guidance has been redefined as a generic helping strategy that encompasses a range of activities of which counselling is one.[2] 'Tutoring' can be used to indicate that the guidance and counselling is provided by tutors, be they personal tutors, course tutors, subject tutors or trainers, as opposed to other specific help provided by specialists such as careers advisers, college counsellors or personal/welfare officers.

Notwithstanding the above, guidance is concerned with the broad range of needs of the individual. The Further Education Unit (FEU) has identified three components:

- Educational Guidance – focused on learning and concerned with matching learning provision to individual learning needs;
- Vocational Guidance – focused on career choice/progression and concerned with facilitating access to, or progression through, employment.
- Personal Guidance – focused on other personal needs and concerned with development of learner self awareness.[3]

Guidance then focuses on the individual's needs within the system. Most teachers and trainers woud accept that any education and training programme should address the needs of the learner. The effectiveness of education and training can be measured in at least three ways:

- By the extent to which it enhances the individual through

qualifications and/or esteem. This requires identifying the individual learner's needs and satisfying them so that each learner is best equipped to achieve and succeed;

- By the extent to which learners understand their learning, are involved in it, and plan and approach it in the most effective way;
- By the extent to which learners develop their own strategies for learning and can use and apply their learning in a continuing variety of circumstances and contexts. In other words, when learners can recognise their own strengths and weaknesses, their learning needs, and take appropriate action to satisfy those needs.

All these criteria are concerned with the 'learner-centredness' of learning and assessment. Further, those responsible for education and training would agree that learning is, more often than not, a social activity. An important part of the learning process is bound up in the learner's awareness of both him or herself and of others.

If education and training is to be more effective then, it must open up the education process and involve the learners actively rather than allocating them the role of passive recipients of teaching. This implies a progressive increase in learner control and autonomy and the learner will need guidance and support during this process. Guidance is thus about enabling people to assess their potential, identify opportunities, increase their awareness of self and others and become responsible for their own lives.[4] Thus those responsible for guidance are concerned to develop these characteristics in the learner. This only comes about by developing the relationship between the individual learner and what is learnt, and often involves developing an appropriate relationship between the learner and the tutor.

In this chapter we shall focus on educational and vocational guidance and shall use the term guidance to include counselling and learning guidance carried out by tutors.

GUIDANCE AND VOCATIONAL EDUCATION AND TRAINING

Guidance is not inherent in learning *per se*, but it can be inherent in the model of teaching and learning operating at any one time. In this sense the 'culture' of existing VET can be defined informally as the guidance systems and arrangements in use. These systems may be inherently embedded in the existing culture of learning and assessment arrangements and systems in a covert, implicit and unrecognised manner. They may be created when learning is organised or takes place over long periods of time. They may evolve surreptitiously or unintentionally without formal recognition.

The current 'culture' of VET may be determined by two general constructs: the existing culture of (i) the organisation and (ii) the learning programme. In FE colleges the culture of the organisation is centred on a federal alliance of departments, and sections where learners are 'owned and protected' through departmental and/or sectional recruitment and responsibility. This construct is strengthened by funding and management arrangements which, for instance, calculate SSRs and allocate staff on a departmental, sectional or course basis. This culture tends to prescribe learning across departments and sections.

The learning programme 'culture' on the other hand, determines the extent to which learners are aggregated into courses with fixed modes of attendance, time bases and so on. Learning takes place in fixed and predetermined locations. Learners are fitted to courses. A single person may have responsibility for almost all aspects of learning. This tends to give rise to guidance systems that are totally integrated with the model of learning in use. Learners know where to go, whom to go to and when to go because of the structure of learning. Efficient systems of guidance can emerge from the predictable and teacher-centred nature of course organisation.

It may be the case that teachers, tutors or trainers do not always recognise that they are involved in guidance. These systems and arrangements may operate quite effectively and efficiently at an informal level. However, they may not be adequate for new forms of learning. There is no guarantee that new forms of learning, which may be less predictable, less formal and constrained and more flexible and diverse will give rise to acceptable systems and arrangements.

New systems of learning and assessment may then require a new approach to guidance. Some have argued that without planning and structuring, adequate forms of guidance will not be produced. This may be particularly important with the NVQ model where learning and assessment are effectively 'decoupled' and can operate independently. Here guidance can provide a coherent underpinning to delivery, helping individuals to monitor their progress and achieve their learning targets.

The experiences of YTS highlight the need for well-designed guidance systems in VET. The importance of those aspects of competence (and learning) that go beyond the job is well know to employers in YTS. There is much evidence from them that the development or acquisition of competence is clouded, or distorted,

without guidance systems that can deal with wider issues.[5] For
example, employers have recognised the need for guidance around
what can be termed the personal needs of a learner:

> One day my trainee seemed to be in a daze; I got quite annoyed and ticked
> him off – his mind wasn't on his work. Later I found out he was worried
> because his father wasn't well.

They have spoken of the need to understand and develop the
relationships between learner and education and training staff:

> Our trainee had only been in England from the West Indies for a few days
> when she came. We had trouble understanding what she was saying. We
> assumed she also couldn't understand us, and took a lot of time and trouble
> explaining every little thing. Later we realised she'd understood everything
> at once, and was very competent in many ways.

They have focused on the need for guiding the learner to take
responsibility for their own learning:

> You have to realise that they don't know things you think are quite natural.
> Like the way to deal with problems when things go wrong. You have to
> stand back and let them try, but be ready to step in, or steer them in the
> right direction. 'Go and see so and so', you might say, when you can see
> they don't know where to turn. Give them a bit of encouragement.[6]

It is worth noting here that the Training Agency argues that the
purpose of guidance in YTS should be to:

> ensure continuing relevance of training and to encourage progress . . . as a
> young person progresses through a . . . programme, that programme will
> become more and more individually tailored to the needs and circumstan-
> ces of the individual. Such a process will not be successful unless adequate
> provision is made for regular guidance and review.[7]

The implementation of NVQs presents a fundamental challenge to
existing vocational education and training structures, processes and
cultures. Traditionally VET has frequently perceived its role in terms
of providing access to teaching. Moreover, this access has been for a
fairly limited clientele, often 16 to 19 year olds, to teaching which is
provided by subject and/or by vocational specialists. Extensive
modifications are required if vocational education and training is to
translate the challenge into relevant and flexible learning and
assessment opportunities for client-learners.

This requires a movement towards a greater availability of a range
of more flexible learning opportunities which are designed to meet the
needs and aspirations of learners of all ages. What is necessary is a shift
in institutional posture and resourcing from being predominantly

provider-led to being learner-led. What is facilitated by National Vocational Qualifications, and is increasingly placed at the centre of institutional planning and implementation is learner-informed curricula. Institutions are now really in the business of learning, not teaching or training. They are moving towards the provision of customised learning programmes designed to meet individual needs and negotiated with the client-learner. In this the role of guidance is paramount.

NEWHAM COMMUNITY COLLEGE: A CASE STUDY

Introduction

Newham Community College is a Group 10 college situated in East London. It is the sole LEA provider of post-16 education and training, with the exception of some GCSE/A level teaching in the Authority's schools. The college has a firm commitment to developing VET, both in the interests of constantly improving the service that the college offers to the community and in the interest of contributing to national work in the system. This latter function has been achieved through the college's involvement in a number of national projects. Amongst these are the TA/NCVQ Accreditation of Prior Learning Project, the TA/FESC Work Based Learning project and the TA/FESC Responsive College Project. The college also has a number of 'in-house' projects around Equity, Flexible Learning and Competence-Led Curricula funded through TA and sponsors its own development projects.

A note on guidance

The Guidance Cycle
While there is a time construct to any process, with Guidance this is not fixed or pre-determined. However many guidance systems revolve around four of the following stages or phases:

- Selection or Pre Entry;
- Induction or Entry;
- Experience, Delivery or During Learning;
- Transition, Progression or End.

The stages are a way of describing what needs to be done. They should not constrain the process. Given individual learning programmes leading to NVQs, these stages are best viewed as a cycle – a cycle that may be completed over periods of time varying from a matter of weeks to a number of years:

The stages in the cycle follow the pattern:

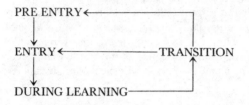

It should be noted that the Transition is most likely to be followed by Entry or Pre-Entry. Of course the learner may immediately leave the formal learning system but this should not be considered as the end of learning. First, learning will almost certainly continue in some informal manner, and second the existence of fallow periods between formal learning stages, no matter how long, does not justify the abrogation of preparation for the next learning stage. Obviously the extent of the preparation may depend upon the anticipated length of time before the next learning stage and the firmness of the learner's decision about what to do and where. In only exceptional circumstances should the Transition stage be seen as the end of the process. It may be that in some circumstances the learner will 'short circuit' the cycle and move from Entry to Transition. This may occur where, for instance, the accreditation of prior learning is absolute and complete.

On a practical note, the most obvious method of ensuring that guidance remains on-going, comprehensive and unconstrained is by the use of regular, planned reviews where demands and need can be identified; action negotiated, agreed and recorded; and the next stage planned. This ensures that the cycle is driven by reviews rather than the anticipation, or assumption, of an end to a linear process.

The Location of Guidance

Two factors are involved here. First, those responsible for guidance should not expect learners to come to them. Guidance will be located as easily in the workplace, library or meeting place, as the providing institution. Decisions about the locations of guidance will have to be made.

Second, attention should be paid to the physical environment in which learning takes place. It should enable and encourage learning. This consideration will in part determine the location and physical environment of guidance. A spectrum of learners will exist, ranging from those who are in effect, 'full time' at the institution to those who will be present only occasionally and not always predictably. This will raise concerns ranging from the physical appearance, function and efficiency of reception areas and sign posting, through the provision of childcare facilities, to the construction of open-plan learning areas. Learners must feel welcome to enter institutions only occasionally, and for a variety of purposes. In short, institutions must be able to cater for a potentially greater number of learners who are spending less time in the institution than has previously been the case.

The Multi-Agency Dimension

While this chapter has concentrated on guidance concerned with learning, it has also recognised the personal dimension of guidance. This personal dimension may not be satisfied solely by individuals employed or located within the institution or its associated learning environments. Indeed, it is likely that there will be a greater need than before to consider the relationships, systems and structures which give rise to a 'multi agency' dimension to guidance – one where institutionally-managed and derived guidance systems are inter-related with other agencies outside the institution and its associated learning environments. This may include agencies such as careers services, personnel officers, social services, and the voluntary sector. This will require 'networking' and is part of any guidance system offered.

The Activities in Guidance

The range of tasks involved in guidance is wide. However, some advice can be given on this aspect of implementing guidance systems by elaborating on the five broad activities identified by Miller[8] and endorsed by others, including the FEU and Training Agency. They are:

1 *Taking action*: For example – organising a work experience placement is part of guidance, especially if a way can be found to help the learner take action for him or herself the next time.
2 *Advising*: For example – suggesting that a learner consults a colleague in the workplace about a specific issue is part of guidance, especially if the learner has the opportunity to disagree with what the colleague says.
3 *Teaching*: For example – setting up a system where the learner can discover his or her own skills, knowledge or competences; or skill, knowledge or competence needs; is part of guidance, especially if the learner is part of the process that identifies the need for this discovery.
4 *Informing*: For example – offering information on the range of

learning styles available is part of guidance, especially if the learners can begin to take action themselves in negotiating their learning.

5 *Counselling*: For example – giving a learner time to explore the feelings of failure, rejection or alienation when an outcome has not been achieved is part of guidance, especially if the learner is better able to deal with these feelings in the future.

It should be stressed that the above listing only begins to describe the broad activities undertaken in maintaining and providing guidance. Longer listings have been identified. In Newham Community College those responsible for guidance carried out an analysis of their own tasks and activities to produce a comprehensive listing. However, it is highly likely that these longer listings are context bound. It would be inappropriate for one institution to 'use' a list derived in another.

A Guidance Code of Practice

Newham Community College Guidance Code of Practice is offered as an example suitable for use in institutions charged with implementing guidance systems and arrangements in support of learning programmes leading to NVQs.

The context of the Guidance Code of Practice
1. Newham Community College exists in order to enable every post-16 member of the community to have access to opportunities to continue with, or return to, further education and training if they so desire.

2. Newham Community College will make it possible for any individual learner, employer or other sponsor, to commission a customised learning programme at any time, and thereby to earn credit through appropriate validating bodies, which will be acceptable, both to employers (via the National Council for Vocational Qualifications) and to further and higher education through access arrangements recognised by the Standing Conference on University Entrance and the Council for National Academic Awards.

3. Newham Community College will therefore uphold and exhibit the recognition and encouragement of diversity. Yet while all client learners will have different needs and aspirations the college will also recognise and implement the entitlement for all of the following community values and principles: the right to equality of access; the right to equality of opportunity; the right to equality of respect; the right to equality of esteem.

4. More specifically, any learner has: the right to assessment,

accreditation and appropriate qualifications; the right to individual learning programmes and appropriate learning resources; the right to learning support, including guidance in the educational, vocational and personal sphere; the right to progression opportunities irrespective of qualifications.

The Guidance Code of Practice

In a learning environment as wide and diverse as Newham Community College, no single model for guidance is applicable for all learners in all contexts. However, a learner's engagement with the college can be framed through the processes of Pre-entry, Entry, During Learning and Transition. In addition, all engagements in these processes recognise that all learning shall be Guidance-supported, Adult-role Focused, Learner-centred and Progression-orientated. Thus for all programmes learners can expect:

- *At pre entry*: Guidance on available learning and progression opportunities in terms of individual needs and aspirations;
- *At entry*: Guidance concerned with orientation and assuming the learning role, initial assessment, and where appropriate, accreditation, and the negotiation and agreement of an individual programme of learning and assessment;
- *During learning*: Guidance on the continued negotiation review and updating of an explicit individual learning programme; the implementation of that programme within an explicit curriculum, access to an individual assessment record, careers advice, personal guidance and access to other agencies as required;
- *On transition*: Guidance on summative assessment and accreditation and in support of the transition to new learning opportunities, the identification and negotiation of appropriate progression routes including an entitlement interview for any NCC programme requested.

An Institutional Framework for Guidance

It is possible to offer a Framework for designing and delivering a guidance system based on the foregoing principles. The formats of the Framework suggests a linear model – one with a 'beginning', a 'middle' and an 'end'. This is simply a result of the format used; the process described by the framework is, as stated above, *cyclical*.

Guidance is not a discrete activity at each stage. It runs through all activities at every stage. The format chosen places guidance under a separate heading at each stage only for the benefit of detail and clarity. Users should reach the guidance activities alongside the Institutional activities identified at each stage. Further, it should be

Figure 7.1 *An institutional framework for guidance*

i Activities in guidance at different stages

PRE ENTRY

MARKETING AND PUBLICITY
- Market research
- Production, co-ordination and distribution of publicity
- Open days/specific on-site events
- Off-site promotional events
- Taster programmers
- Co-ordination of school/industrial/outreach activities

RECEPTION
- Log and respond to all enquiries
- Referral to institution admissions centre
- Referral to/liaison with other organisations/institutions
- Employer/TA etc

QUALITY CONTROL
- Destination analysis
- Target setting
- Log excess/under demand/unfulfilled needs

ENTRY

INITIAL ASSESSMENT
- Interview
- Checking certificated prior learning
- Assessment of prior experience/learning (and where possible accreditation)
- Formal testing
- Diagnostic assessment
- Identification of preferred styles, modes and locations
- Identification of outcomes/accreditation to be achieved
- Identification of additional requirements (Special Learning Needs)

ENROLMENT
- Administrative requirements
- Entry of information on database.

INDUCTION INTO 'THE ROLE OF LEARNER'
- Learner's handbook
- Who's who
- Non learning/assessment facilities/locations

- Learning/study/time management skills
- Learning/assessment locations
- Learning/assessment resources/materials
- Induction into learning/assessment resources materials
- Guidance into learning/assessment resources materials
- Personal guidance support
- Personnel/locations/times/systems

LEARNING CONTRACT/
INDIVIDUAL LEARNING PROGRAMME
formal agreement of learning contract/
individual learning programme covering:

Aims/Objectives;	Methods/Locations;
Resources;	Mode of attendance;
Personnel;	Reviewing arrangements;
Outcomes;	Formal planned assessment/
Progression	accreditation;
arrangements;	Initial calender.

DURING LEARNING

REVIEWS
- Review and updating of individual learning programme
- Ongoing formative and summative assessment
- Compilation, updating and review of learner's portfolio

LEARNING MANAGEMENT
- Management of learning/assessment locations
- Management of learning/assessment resources
- Integration

NETWORKING
- Maintaining learner's access to specialist agencies/personnel (careers/personal support etc)

ACCREDITATION
- Recording of credit accumulation and transfer
- MIS requirements

QUALITY CONTROL

TRANSITION

ACCREDITATION
- Summative assessment
- Accreditation of all competence
- External moderation/validation/awarding arrangements
- Portfolio completion
- Record of achievement
- Credit of achievement
- MIS requirements

EXIT PROGRAMME
- Identification and negotiation of progression route
- References
- Liaison with institutions/organisation offering progression opportunities
- Referral
- Entitlement interview where appropriate

QUALITY CONTROL

---

ii Aspects of guidance

LEARNER'S NEEDS	AIMS OF GUIDANCE	TASKS IN GUIDANCE
PRE ENTRY		
What is on offer? What aspects of myself do I want to develop? How will this help me? What will the opportunity be like? What demands will be made of me?	To help identify learning needs and consider a potential individual learning programme; to help the learner appreciate the inputs, methods, content and outcomes of the opportunity; to help the learner understand the cost/benefits of the opportunity.	Informing Advising Referring Liaising Negotiating Monitoring
ENTRY		
What are my skills/prior experiences? Where is everything Who is everybody? How long have I got? What is expected of me? What have we agreed? How do I get out of here?	To assist the learner in coping with a new experience; to help the learner come to terms with the consequences of his/her decisions; to enable the learner to confront, explore and work through his/her anxiety; to place the learner at the centre of the learning process; to construct and agree the individual learning programme.	Informing Referring Advising Assessing Monitoring Counselling Liaising Contracting
DURING LEARNING		
What have I done? How am I doing? Why do I have to do . . .? Am I happy with my programme? Am I getting what I wanted? What do I have to do next?	to help the learner review and reflect to help the learner face the consequences checking out whether the programme is meeting the contract; being vigilant to the learner's progress and alert to any blocks to learning; recording the learner's progress.	Assessing Coaching Teaching Disciplining Representing Feeding-back Counselling Confronting Referring Monitoring
TRANSITION		
What have I gained? How do I use it? What do I want to do next? What do I need to do about it?	she/he has done; to help the learner examine a range of possible options and choose between them; to help the learner explore the consequences of the options; to help the learner implement action plans; to record achievement.	Assessing Evaluating Counselling Liaising Referring Refereeing

recognised that the listings under the guidance headings at each stage are offered as typical examples only. They are not comprehensive listings.

The Individual Learning Programme (ILP) is' negotiated, compiled, agreed, operationalised, reviewed and recast continuously throughout the process – it is the physical manifestation of the entire set of relationships and processes. It is the means by which guidance (and learning and assessment) is planned, delivered, reviewed and recorded.

The Framework offers a means by which the aims and tasks of guidance together with the institutional activities and learner's needs at each stage, can begin to be identified and integrated together. This Framework enables the institution to be learner-led from the very first and clearly embodies the principle that the elements are not simply grafted onto, and therefore subtractable from, the endeavour to promote learning but are the sustaining heart of the process from which learning opportunities are developed and designed.

Guidance is present at all phases of the process and constitutes an institutional entitlement for all which is Guidance-supported, Adult-role Focused, Learner-centred and Progression-orientated.

Learning Contracts and Individual Learning Programmes

The Individual Learning Programme is the physical manifestation of the set of relationships and processes which make up each individual's programme of learning and assessment. It goes beyond the Learning Contract which has been described as an employer/sponsor-learner-provider triad represented as follows:

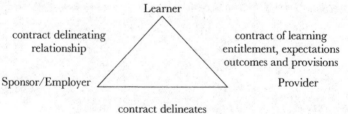

However, this triad must be extended and amended for it to become an Individual Learning Programme. In addition to information included in the contract the Individual Learning Programme would include:

- identified learning needs
- identified prior learning
- aims and objectives of the learning programme, including any expected qualifications
- preferred and agreed learning methods and styles
- mode of attendance
- learning locations, resources and personnel
- reviewing arrangements, both planned and contingency
- assessment and accreditation arrangements
- procedures for recording progress and achievement
- progression expectations
- initial calendar

While each learner will have his or her own Learning Programme, it should not be thought that each learner's programme will be unique in every way. Indeed it may be that significant parts of the programme are identical to the programmes of other learners. Similarly the possession of an Individual Learning Programme does not indicate that all learning takes place alone. The virtues and benefits of group learning are to be protected. Individual Learning Programmes should recognise this. Care has to be taken in designing a suitable format. Often these formats will hold information not only for learning and guidance purposes but also for Management Information System (MIS) purposes. Various pilot formats exist. Some have been adapted from YTS and Individual Action Plan used by ET, others have their roots in Pre-Vocational Education courses such as CPVE. More original formats have been developed by other organisations and national projects. Amongst them are formats developed by the TA/FESC Work-based Learning Project and the TA/NCVQ Accreditation of Prior Learning Project.

Staff and institutional implications

Developments in VET have tended to be initiated by changes in, or the introduction of, specific schemes. However, in the past, these changes have, either by design or in effect, been confined to only parts of the institution's curricula. This has been the case with, for instance, the introduction of CPVE and YTS. Two general, inter-related, features characterise these past experiences.

First, institutions have not been required to respond across the institution to these developments. In fact these developments have left the majority of VET provision unaffected and unchanged. Without any intention of diminishing the value and strength of CPVE it is true to state that in many institutions the introduction and development of CPVE has been marginal to VET provision and may well have taken place without any reference to some vocational sectors. Certainly staff involved only with specific validating bodies, for example BTEC or City and Guilds, will have been little involved in CPVE.

Second, it has been possible for curriculum development to precede staff development and for staff development to precede institutional development. Further, the change and development required at each stage of this process has diminished. While major curriculum development has taken place, only some staff development has been required and this has in turn demanded only limited institutional development. In part this characteristic has been informed by the first. The absence of the need for cross-institution response has justified changes focused primarily on curriculum development, only secondarily on staff development and with only minimal, and perhaps marginal, institutional development.

This model of changes has been described as:

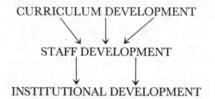

This model will not be adequate for the introduction of NVQs. Institutional responses to NVQs will need to be across the institution since the impact of NVQs will have an effect on all VET and all validating bodies. While there can be no doubt that significant curriculum development will be required, there is equally little doubt that the impact on staff roles and institutional structures will be great. Further, institutions will recognise that curriculum development may not be possible without institutional development. The FEU have suggested that a process capable of responding to change of this order might be described by the following diagram.[9]

This approach to organisational change embodies characteristics suitable for changes required in response to the introduction of NVQs. Curriculum development, staff development, and institutional development are both inter-related and synchronised. This enables each element to support the other two and is more appropriate to a cross institution response. This approach also enables each issue in learning and assessment to be considered in relation to all aspects of the institution. This approach is required where institutions are considering guidance arrangements, organisation and systems.

Staff Development
There can be little doubt that the changes in guidance systems required by the introduction of competence-led programmes of learning leading to NVQs will demand new roles and functions for staff.

In some institutions, such as ET and YTS training establishments, existing staff roles may already include some who have formal responsibilities which can be adapted to take on the greater demands of guidance required by those new programmes. YTS liaison officers already have responsibilities for negotiating the learning programme with the learner and for co-ordinating learning, separately from providing it. Liaison officers may also take on guidance functions so ensuring that, together with teacher and trainers, a range of guidance services are provided to, and for, the learner.

In colleges, especially for full-time learners, existing arrangements may be the sole responsibility of teaching staff. It is no criticism of these staff to recognise that college teachers often consider their primary role to be providers of knowledge, understanding, skills and experience. This is not to deny that college staff do not take guidance seriously, nor to deny that guidance systems exist. It is to argue that in these cases guidance arrangements and systems may be embedded, informally, in the culture of the existing learning provision. The establishment of new roles and functions, in these cases, may require more than the simple amendment of some existing job descriptions. It is not suggested that the roles and functions of all staff will change, but it may be necessary for institutions to create new staff roles – roles that are more concerned with the formal and explicit provision of services such as guidance, than with the direct and exclusive provision of learning.

Whatever the existing pattern of arrangements, institutions face a number of tasks in relation to responding to the implications for staff of the introduction of competence-led programmes of learning leading to NVQs. These tasks may include:

- the mapping or auditing of existing, perhaps unrecognised, staff guidance expertise;
- a needs analysis of staff at all levels involved in providing and/or managing guidance systems and arrangements;
- the negotiation of individual action plans for staff and course teams;
- the derivation of institution-devised learning units, to enable the achievement of action plan objectives and the satisfaction of training needs;
- the provision of 'drop in' staff development workshops;
- providing access to externally validated awards (eg: RSA Diploma in counselling);
- the (re)training of staff as specialist guidance staff;
- use of FEU, RAC/RCB, OU, and NCVQ Staff Development Guidelines, Networks and Training Packs;
- the (re)training of staff in skills to lead, support, co-ordinate and provide these initiatives.

Institutional Development

If a cross-institution response to the new programmes of learning leading to NVQs is to be enabled and curriculum, staff and institutional development are to be mutually supportive and synchronised, then institutions need to plan their institutional development. However, the truth is, that institutions, as yet have little experience of the kind of mechanisms required. As one Vice Principal of a large college put it 'This is foreign land for colleges at the moment'.

Despite this, it is possible to identify institutional approaches appropriate to the implementation of learning and guidance systems leading to NVQs. In this identification of approaches, Newham Community College is used as a 'case study'.

i Planning change

Institutions will need to devise clear objectives for the new systems. This will involve explicit and public policy statements, for coherent and operational codes of practice and the establishment of institutional systems and structures to support curriculum changes and deliver staff development.

ii Policy statement

At NCC a 'mission statement' has been used which articulates the mission of the college for the next three years. This has not only set objectives and outcomes to be achieved over the period but has also had the effect of galvanising the staff and making them feel part of the

process of change. In this respect the statement has had a valuable
dissemination function. This statement also has uses in marketing the
college to the community. Obviously the statement informs, and is
informed by, other planning activities. The statement has been
produced by the principal, advised and supported by the 'Learning
for Yourself' working group made up of senior staff and activity
managers, chaired by a Vice Principal. This Working Group has
commissioned investigations into the college curriculum.

From the point of view of guidance the statement has described the
intended model, or culture, of learning and assessment. This in turn
has led to an examination of the learning styles, client groups and
resource requirements of the new programmes of learning and
assessment. Thus it is possible to begin to identify the kind of guidance
systems which will be required.

iii *Funding and co-ordinating agents of change*

The establishment of a Development Fund signalled the corporate
recognition of the need for a budgetary mechanism to enable the
college to plan and respond to change. A fund of a significant number
of hours with a set of criteria was established. Groups, departments,
and teams bid for support from this fund on the basis of the criteria.
The criteria for the 89/90 year included individual learning programmes, appropriate guidance support systems, pre-entry guidance
programmes and staff development activities necessary to prepare for,
and deliver competence-led curricula.

In this way change was encouraged and enabled throughout the
college, including those changes orientated on the establishment of
new guidance systems. The establishment of the criteria by senior
management assured the institutional development was synchronised
with the curriculum and staff development and was commensurate
with the 'learning for yourself' 'mission' of the college.

iv *Co-ordination of change*

A cross-college response clearly demands cross-college co-ordination.
NCC now has in post a number of cross-college activity managers and
medium term project initiatives corresponding to the managers and
medium term project initiatives corresponding to the learning,
assessment and guidance cycle. In addition to those organisations
mentioned above, notably the 'Learning For Yourself' Working
Group and the guidance Task Group, the college established working
parties on Progression and Admissions and participated in major
research projects looking at APL, the Responsive College, Flexible
and Work-based Learning and Equity. NCC have also made new

appointments of an NVQ Co-ordinator, and three Directors of Open Learning, Marketing and Assessment.

While only one working group has been concerned exclusively with guidance, many of the college project co-ordinators have tackled issues of, or in, guidance. For instance, the APL Project has been concerned with producing formats and guidelines for the compilation of the Individual Working Party and the Admissions Working Party, the Equity Project has considered the role of guidance in learning; the NVQ Co-ordinator has identified guidance as a major development area in the implementation of NVQs. Indeed, it has been argued that there is a virtue in not leaving guidance solely to one group, project or member of staff. By expecting a variety of groups, projects and members of staff to consider guidance, guidance is not 'ghettoised' or allowed to be excluded from any of the central concerns of the institution – guidance is maintained as a central fact of all learning and assessment.

v *Embedding change*

Institutions need to consider how change will be embedded. The Development Fund and the cross-institution staff have an important role here, but NCC has considered other, additional methods:

CODES OF PRACTICE A Guidance Task Group, composed from college experts and chaired by a Head of Department was given the task, and the funding, to devise a Guidance Code of Practice. This Task Group drew on published documents, examples of good practice, both formal and informal, within the college and without. It was concerned not to produce an abstract idealised document, but one that was derived from existing arrangements and which was capable of being developed further through use. Equally, it took full account of the 'Learning for Yourself' policy statement setting out the 'mission' for the college.

COURSE TEAMS An overhaul of Course Teams is required. Course Teams need to set up new systems of, and arrangements for, guidance. If Course Teams set their own development plans, within policy objectives, support can be provided and Course Teams become a genuine part of the development process.

REVIEW OF ORGANISATION Certain aspects of institutional organisation may need reviewing. This may not be so much a case of devising brand new organisational structures as considering whether the criteria for past decisions still exists. For instance, the range of college organisational models is well known, including, as it does matrix and departmental models. Colleges have chosen which model to adopt for good reasons. However, the criteria which informed those decisions may no longer be valid. Certainly colleges may wish to review the relationship between groups, departments, units or teams with the new criteria of enabling a greater degree of flexibility and cross-college learning programmes. Any guidance system will clearly be informed by these decisions. Perhaps more critically, these structural decisions may have to be made on the basis of the needs of guidance requirements.

The use of resources such as workshops may need to be reviewed. At NCC this provision has been reviewed with the purpose of co-ordinating workshop learning and assessment more closely and investigating the possibility of giving learners access to workshops in pursuit of learning programmes outside a course. There are important implications for guidance systems here since colleges will require guidance systems capable of operating outside courses but integrating workshop provision with individual learners needs.

vi *New college structures*
It is apparent that institutions may have to consider new structures. Two initiatives at NCC have been considered in this respect, in part, responding to the need for new structures capable of offering guidance in new ways. The Customer Services Unit was set up to provide an all year capacity for effective advice on college provision and offers advice and referral for all customers, be they sponsors (employers) and/or learners. The unit also monitors the effectiveness of the service, markets courses to the community and seeks to establish income generating links with local sponsors.

The rationale of the Admissions Unit was explained by a Vice Principal:

> On entry to college, students need a radically different admissions procedure, not on the basis of 36 weeks a year, but from the basis of an all-year service. Admissions for curriculum purposes asks students where they start from, where they want to go and how (the college and associated learning and assessment environments) can help them get there. This requires a new recording system to facilitate the recording of credit accumulation and transfer. (Colleges) need systems that will map learning as well as map the accreditation of the learning process. So admission takes on a completely new focus – the curriculum. It forms the hub of the wheel from which all activities radiate.[10]

vii *Management Information Systems (MIS)*
There is a need to consider new forms of MIS. Guidance systems may need access to a far wider range of information and management may require those responsible for guidance, to have access to college

information in the absence of more traditional means of collecting such information.

vii *Staff development*
Staff Development is dealt with fully in another section of this document. However, institutions may need to consider the funding and organisation of Staff Development. This may include establishment of Staff Development priorities, its co-ordination with LERATGs priorities and WRNAFE categories, the desired outcomes of Staff Development programmes and the fitting of staff to specialist programmes.

ix *Costings, fees and SSRs*
Institutions will need to consider the cost of implementing new systems and structures. Decisions will have to be made about the fees charged to learners who do not require the traditional course. Further, new systems will have consequences for the calculation and/ or interpretation of SSRs.

Mapping learning and assessment

Guidance supports learning and assessment. Those responsible for guidance will need to know what form learning and assessment is to take for each learner in order to ensure that guidance does support learning and assessment. In addition the learner will want to know what modes, methods and styles are available. Those responsible for planning guidance systems will need to 'uncover' existing guidance arrangements, yet these existing arrangements may be embedded in existing learning arrangements. All this points to the need for a mapping of learning and assessment. The de-coupling of learning from assessment will place a greater emphasis on mapping of this sort. This mapping may well contribute to the design and compilation of Individual Learning Programmes.

Mapping the Flexibility of Learning
It should not be assumed that all existing provision is inflexible. Rather, mapping tends to suggest that a degree of flexibility exists in conventional, or traditional, learning schemes and courses. This flexibility may, indeed, be unrecognised or covert. However, it may be these factors which determine existing implicit guidance systems and arrangements. Mapping will enable planners to 'uncover' existing guidance arrangements. In fact in some cases it will enable planners to discover very adequate systems and preserve them for future use as learning is reconstructed.

It should also not be assumed that the greatest degree of flexibility is always, or even usually, required or desirable. Enhancing flexibility is concerned with extending learner choice, autonomy and control. In this respect it has similar aims (although different methods) to guidance. Enhancing flexibility clearly alters the relationship between the learner and and the learning process. However, if enhancing flexibility begins to reduce the degree of support given to the learner, without good reason, or to disrupt or complicate the relationship between the learner and the process of learning, then furthering flexibility is a pedagogic fault, not a virtue. This observation underlines the crucial relationship between learning and guidance.

Birch and Latcham's dimensions of flexibility provide a basis for mapping.[11] They include mode of attendance, duration of programme, learning resources, learning location, and learning style. It should be recognised that although spectrums of flexibility can be described, for instance from 'no choice' to 'negotiable outside specified curriculum to meet students' needs' for 'aims and content', Birch and Latcham do not prescribe points on each spectrum that are desirable. This is for providers to determine through negotiation with all parties concerned.

While these dimensions provide a suitable starting point for any mapping, users should recognise that the terrain of VET in 1983, when the dimensions were developed, was rather different to the terrain of VET in the 1990s. Birch and Latcham assumed (p 5) that 'students are conventionally formed onto courses'. While this was a perfectly valid assumption in 1983, it will prove inadequate in the 1990s. Therefore, those engaged in responding to new initiatives will need to adapt, develop, extend and apply these measures to learning programmes, or potential 'navigations', rather than 'courses'. This is all the more important where guidance is concerned. Further, those responsible for guidance will be at least as interested in *what* the learner wants from the engagement with the institution as *how* the institution can respond once the engagement commences.

One approach to this issue is to consider Birch and Latcham's dimensions as one axis of a matrix. The other axis can be described first, by classifying the broad purpose of the learner's need as either primarily vocational/occupational or non vocational or of self discovery only (learner self interest). One can then proceed by further analysing the learner's requirements in terms of access issues, including access to learning experiences and/or materials, teaching, learning support and/or guidance, assessment and/or self assessment and to a qualification and/or qualification units. This approach enables a learning map to be produced which categorises learners' requirements and matches them with the institution's responses. This enables the needs of guidance to be identified within the learning programme.

Mapping Progress and Achievement
Progress can be differentiated from achievement by reference to the following example: a learner attempts a unit of competence but is judged 'not competent'. Is this recorded simply as a 'failed attempt'? Is it not possible that the learner was 'competent' in some elements and even 'nearly competent' in others (eg: could type at 45wpm with 10 per cent accuracy compared with the standard which demanded 50wpm with 5 per cent accuracy). Equally is it not possible that the learner has improved their performance over time without performing to standard? (eg: the learner was only managing 30wpm with 20 per cent accuracy a month ago).

What is at issue here is formative assessment. Yet the assessment of NVQs cannot always, if ever, be predetermined as formative or summative. As a rule of thumb: if the learner is competent then the assessment is summative, if the learner is not competent then the assessment is formative. This generates a need for guidance. Learners may need to reflect, review, replan their learning. This process is very much tied up with the individual's learning programme. The obvious vehicle for guidance here, is the Individual Learning Programme (ILP) review: review must follow all assessment, in addition to any other planned, or unplanned, reviews.

NCVQ's National Record of Vocational Achievement provides a common means of recording achievement and accumulating the units/credits towards NVQs and other national qualifications. The National Record also contains a facility for providers to build in methods of recording progress. It can thus play an active role in formative assessment, although it is often regarded purely as a vehicle for summative recording. If NROVA is to lead to a rationalisation of recording procedures within qualifications, the status and functions of its sections will need to be outlined in greater detail.

Methods of Assessment and Guidance
Assessment through performance to standards has many implications. Assessment may take place in the workplace, learners may collect evidence of performance over time and from a variety of locations and may present it for judgement at a later date in an entirely new location. Guidance systems will be required that can span these time periods and locations. Further, those responsible for guidance may

need to know *how* the evidence was collected, *who* collected it, the *context* of the collection and so on. Where the learner has collected evidence prior to engaging with the institution, staff will have to be able to interrogate this assessment information. Where evidence has been collected, and judgements made, as part of a programme, staff require knowledge of both what should happen and what did happen – the planned method. All this requires guidance systems that can map the actual collection and judgement of evidence for assessment, identify and agree how future assessment information should be collected and judged and compare the two. This demands assessment mapping-systems to map the flow of information, the stages in the assessment process, the locations, personnel and contents of assessment and the criteria necessary for accreditation. Various methods of assessment mapping have been developed by various bodies and projects including the TA/FESC Work-based Learning Project.

REFERENCES

1 Morris, B. 'Guidance as a Concept in Educational Philosophy' in *Yearbook of Education*, 1955.
2 Miller, J. 'Tutoring', FEU, 1982.
3 *'Personal Guidance Bases'*, FEU, 1988.
4 'Challenge of Change', UDACE, 1986.
5 McCoy, S. 'Supporting Quality in YTS', FEU, 1989.
6 Silver, R. & Grubb Institute, 'Personal Effectiveness – Practitioners' Guide', MSC, 1987.
7 'Development of the Youth Training Scheme', MSC, 1985.
8 Miller, op. cit.
9 'Implementing New Vocational Qualifications', FEU, 1988.
10 Silver, R. Transcript of speech to NCVQ, TA APL Conference, 1988.
11 Birch, D. & Latcham, J. 'Flexible Learning in Action', FEU, 1984.

8. Students with special needs

David Hutchinson

INTRODUCTION

The reform and rationalisation of the national system of vocational qualifications are likely to be of benefit to all students, especially students with special needs. The advantages of the new system of credit accumulation and the National Record of Vocational Achievement (NROVA) which merit attention as likely to be of particular benefit to students with special needs are:

- Easier access to qualifications;
- Units can be built up over time;
- Students can be motivated by the immediate recognition of their achievements;
- Different parts of a learning programme and different modes of learning can be integrated;
- More flexible learning programmes can be designed;
- A clear statement of the student's competence can be made in language familiar to an employer.

However, many students with special needs have disabilities of mind and body which present difficulties in the learning environment. It is often those difficulties which become the focus of attention rather than the abilities possessed by the individual. This has implications for the education and training of young people with special needs and there is general agreement in the field that such young people often leave school less well educated, and less well trained than their able-bodied peers.

The report, *Handicapped Youth at Work*[1] suggests, in this context that 'the low standards and expectations of special schools and the lack of effective teaching in mainstream schools is equally unsatisfactory and both represent a failure to assist young people in their development and serve to limit their life chances.' This has resulted in many young people with special needs reaching the end of their school years less well equipped with basic vocational and technical skills to enter the labour market than their able-bodied colleagues. As a consquence they have a higher unemployment rate than able-bodied leavers. A survey, undertaken by the National Children's Bureau on behalf of the Warnock Committee of Enquiry into the Education of Handicapped Children and Young People,[2] revealed an unemployment rate among disabled school-leavers of 19.1 per cent as compared to 4.4 per cent among the non-disabled. All of this has denied to some young people with special needs the basic psychological functions which work offers. The report, *Disabled Youth: A Right to Adult Status*[3] lists these as:

- personal identity;
- self-esteem;
- responsibility;
- dignity;
- acceptance of others.

The whole rôle of the disabled person in society is problematic. Disability, as an equal opportunities issue, has never been an issue of central public concern in the same way as race and gender. There are many negative images of disability. Stereotyping to the detriment of the disabled person exists. Indeed the words that are used, 'impairment' 'disability', and 'handicap' are not well understood. They are often used interchangeably as though synonymous. The World Health Organisation offers the following definitions:[4]

Impairment: any loss or disability of psychological, physiological ·or anatomical structure or function.

Disability: any restriction or lack (resulting from an impairment) of ability to perform an activity in the manner or within the range considered normal for a human being.

Handicap: a disadvantage for a given individual, resulting from an impairment or disability, that limits or prevents the fulfilment of a role that is normal, depending on age, sex, social and cultural factors for that individual.

It is clear, in the field of vocational education and training, that impairment and disability will present difficulties for the individuals involved. What we should be concerned with, at the outset, is that impairment and disability do not become a handicap as a result of the environment within which the individual finds him or herself.

The National Council for Vocational Qualifications, writing on access and equal opportunities in relation to NVQs, stated:[5]'it is the aim of the National Council to secure the delivery of a framework which will promote equal opportunities for those who have special needs . . .' The definition of 'special needs' has to recognise, therefore, that there is a wide range of people, possibly with learning difficulties, physical or sensory disabilities, emotional or behaviour problems and any combination of these, who may need some special help in acquiring vocational qualifications on an occasional, or, perhaps, continuous basis.

SPECIAL NEEDS IN GENERAL

Reference has already been made above to the use of certain terms in association with disabling conditions. Very often phrases such as 'suffering from Spina-Bifida' appear in a student's record as if he or she had recently contracted a contagious disease, again reinforcing the medical model of disability. Moreover, people with a particular disability are often grouped together under a generic heading usually prefaced with the word 'the', for example 'the blind', 'the deaf', 'the mentally handicapped', 'the epileptic'.

This is a dangerous practice which can lead to the assumption, in the minds of the uninformed, that the people grouped together in this way will present a homogeneous set of needs. Nothing can be further from the truth. Unfortunately, there are many well-publicised examples of decisions which have been made over the lives of disabled people based on these uniform stereotypes. It is important, therefore, that the needs of every disabled person entering training are assessed on an individual basis, taking into account those factors which are relevant to that individual.

Physical/sensory/medical problems

Students with these problems may very well be able to participate in mainstream training programmes on an integrated basis but may require the provision of some special resources and/or facilities, for example, help with access to buildings and/or rooms, special aids and equipment, aids to communication, care staff support, adapted methods of teaching/instruction, together with modifications to assessment procedures.

Learning difficulties

Learning difficulties (or difficulties in the learning process) may manifest themselves in a variety of ways and range from those students with very mild difficulties who have been educated in a mainstream setting with some remedial help, possibly in the basic subjects of English and mathematics, to those students with severe intellectual impairment who have been educated in a very special environment.

It is both difficult and dangerous to generalise about such students. Nevertheless it has to be recognised that some young people will not be capable of achieving any type of vocational qualification and require placements post-school which will not involve any form of work. Equally many young people who have moderate learning difficulties have found it difficult to gain access to training opportunities but they could achieve creditable results if given appropriate help and support.

Many such students have difficulty in generalising from their learning and cannot transfer what has been learned in one situation to another. Repeated opportunities to practise new skills may overcome this problem. The student's rate of learning may be slower than his or her more able peers but he or she can very often reach the same standard given more time. Flexible allocation of time is therefore important.

Students with learning difficulties often find the use of language is a problem, especially if the language in question is unnecessarily complicated. Reducing the language used in training situations to its simplest possible form without distorting meaning will be of help, not only to students with special needs but to all learners.

The fact that students with learning difficulties may have experienced repeated failure in the past may cause them to show lack of confidence or to be unwilling to subject themselves to further humiliation. Training schedules which are broken down into easily achievable steps can help the student to overcome these problems and enhance his or her self-confidence and self-respect.

Specific learning difficulties

Specific learning difficulties are a more recently identified set of problems usually associated with localised learning difficulties. It is important that specific learning difficulties are not confused with the more generalised learning difficulties described above. Very often students with specific learning difficulties will have average or above average ability but may experience problems with oral expression, written expression, spelling, reading, arithmetic, memory, concentration and perceptional-motor dysfunction such as poor handwriting, confusion of left and right and writing or reading some letters or numbers backwards. One hopes that such students will have had their particular difficulty diagnosed while still at school and that they will have received appropriate help and support. Nevertheless, the problem may remain to some extent into adulthood and this can be greatly helped by sensitive counselling and support together with the provision of special help in the particular area of weakness.

Emotional, behavioural or psychiatric problems

There are students who have some emotional, behavioural or psychiatric problem which will affect their capacity to work and learn. The range of problems presented is extremely diverse, is not necessarily related to ability and is likely to extend across the whole student population. Young people who have had these problems at school may have received some form of special education and be labelled 'maladjusted'. Their difficulties may extend beyond school and be indicated by a sense of failure and rejection which can lead to the vicious circle of disaffected behaviour repeating itself.

Adults with psychiatric problems, on the other hand, may be very highly motivated but may be under- or over-confident, which may show in problems of concentration and disturbed behaviour. Attendance at college may provide, for the first time, an opportunity for the student to undergo a positive learning experience. It is important that colleges recognise this and provide a welcoming environment together with the resources to provide the amount of support required.

SPECIAL NEEDS AND NVQs

What are the general implications of the involvement of students with special needs on programmes leading to NVQs? What issues and principles do they pose for consideration?

The presence of a disability in a particular student does not necessarily mean that she or he will have special educational needs. By the time the young person leaves school the difficulties they may have experienced in the past may have been overcome or, at least, bypassed. Equally some students will have significant special educational needs which will make progress towards desired objectives problematic.

In the past it has often been the case that these problems have been insurmountable, largely through lack of understanding of the problems and the unavailability of the necessary support. Today the situation may have improved in both respects, but it has to be recognised that, even with support, students with special needs will have to work harder and longer than their able-bodied peers in order to obtain the same vocational qualifications. This problem can be alleviated if all educational organisations, together with validating bodies, adopt a common approach.

General principles

No concessions should be sought in the setting of standards. Indeed, as indicated in NCVQ Information Leaflet No. 3[6]: 'There is no question that the standards required in employment as specified in the performance criteria for qualifications, should be lowered to promote an equal opportunities policy for those with special needs. This would serve no purpose and destroy the credibility of NVQs generally.'

Nevertheless, positive commitment on the part of all those agencies concerned in programme development, and a flexibility of approach, are key features which will promote the achievement of those standards. The outcomes reached by addressing the particular requirements of students with special needs is more than likely to enhance the quality of provision for all students. The areas where problems are most frequently encountered by students with special needs are: the range of qualifications available, selection criteria, curriculum and evaluation methodology, and resources.

The range of qualifications

Information Leaflet No. 3 suggests that 'candidates with special needs should be encouraged to pursue qualifications and units of competence in which they have a reasonable chance of attaining the required standard.' However, in selecting programmes or units that will form part of an NVQ, it is important that the range of essential skills required by employers is considered. Sufficient and appropriate qualifications are necessary to reflect these skills, since a large proportion of the workforce will be excluded from gaining qualifications when the entire range of skills is not considered.

Students with learning difficulties are often disadvantaged in this way as there are insufficient qualifications available which are achievable. Learning which goes unrecognised can result in frustration for both the learner and the teacher and can be a waste of valuable resources when there is no apparent goal or outcome.

There is clear evidence of the need for innovation in this important area where both the scope and breadth of possible qualifications is improved. Of particular significance are those schemes which are looking towards the introduction of preparatory awards which can provide the necessary stepping stones towards the achievement of a recognised NVQ for many students with special needs.

Selection criteria

Students with special needs will be referred to further education from a variety of agencies. For example: the careers service, the disablement resettlement service, social services departments and voluntary organisations. There often exists a confusion as to exactly what does or does not constitute a special educational need. This inconsistency can be brought about by the differences in understanding that exist between schools and colleges and the different agencies concerned. Rather than bringing about a general understanding, the implementation of the 1981 Education Act[7] has been affected by non-educational factors such as finance.

It is to be expected that the implementation of the 1988 Education Act will bring similar problems. When the Youth Training Scheme (YTS) was first introduced in the 1980s, the definition of special needs which was used was narrow and served largely to limit rather than enhance opportunities.[8] As a result of considerable pressure from organisations concerned with the education and training of young people with special needs, the definitions used within the YTS were revised and became more all-embracing.[9] If history is not to repeat itself, then more precisely yet broadly applicable definitions of special needs should be used in the development of NVQs.[10]

In developing a procedure for addressing special educational needs, the following principles should be followed:

1 Skills and abilities should be identified, not merely prior academic attainment and qualifications. Restricted educational opportunities and prolonged periods of absence, for example, may have prevented students with special needs from achieving certain 'milestone' qualifications, but they may have acquired the prerequisite skills by informal education and learning.
2 Potential problems, and possible solutions, should be identified before the start of a programme of education/training, not once it is underway. The young person concerned should be fully involved in this process.
3 A longer than usual period of assessment should be allowed for. The complex problems often presented by students with special needs cannot be managed by rigid adherence to a set procedure. Information from a variety of agencies and sources may be required in order to deal effectively with the needs presented by the student.

4 Selection should be made on the basis of the information and data available through observation and by interview of the young person him- or herself. Speculative assumptions should not be allowed to enhance the level of disability.

Curriculum and evaluation methodology

Achieving an NVQ is not necessarily beyond the abilities of a young person with special educational needs. If the college or training organisation and the validating body adopt an attitude directed towards promoting success; if they develop, and provide procedures and structures facilitating success, then their students with special educational needs can achieve the same outcome as their able-bodied peers. Too often, however, a very significant barrier to achieving vocational qualifications is created for people with special needs, by the particular methods and conditions of testing skills which can sometimes unnecessarily prevent success, especially for people with physical and sensory disabilities.

The following steps can do much to remove the limitations imposed:

1 Identify precisely:
  - the competence;
  - the conditions for demonstrating the competence;
  - the criteria that measure performance of the competence.
2 Identify the situations in which it is impossible to alter any or all of the conditions.
3 Identify a range of alterations or adaptations that can be made in order to allow a student with special educational needs to acquire competence.
4 Assess the achievement of competence within a range of conditions or criteria so that the student can achieve success measured within that range. This will vary in specific ways for specific skills. What must be constant is the recognition that the usual methods for demonstrating competence are not the only ways.
5 Allow for a variety of learning styles to be used to develop the same competences.
6 Establish priorities among the competences or identify a sequence for acquiring the competences that will result in a flexible time-frame. This will allow a person with special educational needs to learn at a slower pace than is usual but still to accumulate different competences which will result in a qualification.

Resources

In the development of programmes for students with special needs leading to the acquisition of NVQs, the following resource implications will have to be considered:

1 It is essential for the student with special needs to be offered the appropriate counselling support both before and during a programme.
2 Increased teacher/student involvement may be necessary.
3 Physical access may need to be facilitated, the provision of specialist equipment or equipment adaptation may be required.
4 Development of the procedures for increasing the flexibility of the curriculum and evaluation methodology, and for responsiveness to individual needs, may be required.

These resource implications may require the development of procedures for gaining access to various government-sponsored funds, grants and non-traditional sources of revenue if the education and training of students with special needs is to be effective.

The attainment of a recognised NVQ is of advantage to the student in particular and to the national workforce in general. The introduction of flexible approaches to gaining a qualification is advantageous to all students, not just to those with special educational needs, and the ultimate goals of both education and training will be served. The result will be people who function effectively in their chosen occupation or role.

RESPONDING TO SPECIAL NEEDS

The resolution of the difficulties faced by students with special needs involved in programmes leading to the award of an NVQ will not rest solely with the new procedures introduced in the NVQ framework, important as these may be. Many of the difficulties will have solutions at the level of the local provider of education and training.

The flexibility which is inherent in the philosophy of the NCVQ, and in the practices outlined for equality of opportunity, will benefit the young person with special needs only if providers themselves are adaptable and innovative in implementing the new systems, and if they develop a positive policy and strategy for providing appropriately for these young people.

The systems necessary for providing a good service for students with special needs will also benefit large numbers of other, non-disabled students. Special needs are but a continuum of ordinary needs. Any attention paid to special needs, therefore, should be within the general context of the enhancement of competence for all students and special needs will be firmly embedded in this overall philosophy.

In *Descriptions, Definitions and Directions: Special Needs in Further and Continuing Education*[11], John Fish argues for a new definition of special needs. This moves away from the labelling of the learner (in a disabled category) to the listing of support needs. Thus 'special' is defined as the 'special support that certain learners need to succeed in their learning'. A warning is given of the capacity, which is present, potentially, in every organisation, to be a 'handicapping influence'. The education/training institution can influence a young person's life by the expectations that it has for him or her, the type of provision that it offers and the procedures by which it operates: 'A college . . . can either compound society's handicapping effect on the individual learner or help to liberate them from it.'

It is possible to meet special needs in many different ways. However, the extent to which special needs can be met in an education/training situation is often a good indication of the flexibility of that situation and the range of support that is provided. John Fish categorised the strategies needed as:

1 'Extending ways in which learning can take place;
2 Extending the range of individual variation lecturers can teach effectively in classes;
3 Providing individual counselling and support.'

Now a fourth category needs to be added. Finding alternative methods of assessing for competence.

Extending ways in which learning can take place

The development of an education/training programme is a complex business with many different interrelationships. It is likely that programmes leading to the award of an NVQ will have an emphasis at the design stage on standards set by the appropriate LIB. As such it may be thought that such programmes will be 'unfriendly' to those who have special needs. This will indeed be the case if suitable alternative strategies are not put in place to make possible the achievement of a qualification, and at the same time maintain the standards of performance required by industry and commerce.

Providing flexible learning opportunities for students with special needs and meeting the standards of performance set by industry and commerce might seem irreconcilable objectives. In *Flexible Learning Opportunities and Special Educational Needs*[12] Deborah Cooper, discussing the process of learning, suggests that the mode of learning be so organised as to fit in with the needs of the individual rather than the institution and that the learning process should be taken to the learner if this is required to meet individual needs. If students with special needs are to take advantage of the new flexibility afforded by the system of NVQs then this message of providing facilities for independent but directed study must be heeded by colleges and other providers of education and training.

There are many examples of open learning, flexi-study, part-time and outreach schemes which have been developed to meet the needs of a wide group of clients, not just those whith special needs, for whom attendance at, and accessibility to, a college under traditional regimes is not possible. Such initiatives will need to be encouraged further if the objective of the NCVQ is to ensure that: 'access to qualifications is opened up by the removal of unnecessary restrictions on methods and periods of learning . . .'[13]

Many students with special needs who are faced with problems of access and attendance at colleges, due to a wide variety of either permanent or temporary difficulties, will require these adjustments in order to acquire qualifications. To assist colleges in assessing their ability to meet these demands, the following checklist has been compiled using the suggestions given in *Flexible Learning Opportunities and Special Educational Needs*.

1 Are alternative learning methods available, eg open learning, distance-learning, flexi-study, drop-in facilities, outreach provision and other modes of attendance?
2 Is a range of resources/facilities available to support alternative learning methods, including support systems for students?
3 Can students begin a programme of study at any time during the year?
4 Are modular learning packages available which allow students as much time as they need to complete individual units of study?

Extending the range of individual variation lecturers can teach effectively in classes

All students are individuals and as such have individual needs, interests and abilities which affect their performance in the learning/training situation. It is important that the teacher identifies the requirements of each individual and recognises these in the planning and provision of education/training. This is something which is true for all learners. It is even more so with learners who have special educational needs.

Traditionally learner-centredness has not been a characteristic of the route to the acquisition of vocational qualifications. Indeed the very opposite has often been the case, where not only the content of programmes, but, more important, the mode of delivery has been subject to only marginal change by awarding and validating bodies. If students with special needs are to benefit from the new NVQ framework, then the system for acquiring qualifications must be both accessible to all and be based on the acquisition of competence no matter how it was acquired.

These objectives will be achieved for all learners, including those with special needs, only if a learner-centred approach is used. This focuses attention on the individual teacher who will need to ask him- or herself the following key questions as suggested by Faraday and Harris in *Learning Support*:[14]

- Am I treating the learner as an individual?
- Do I understand what learner-centredness means?
- Do I understand the relationship between:
  (a) Learner-centredness
  (b) Individual learning programmes?
- Have I the knowledge and techniques to recognise individual needs?
- Can I respond to individual needs?
- Can I produce an individual learning programme?

Responding to these challenges will require a good deal of reappraisal and reorientation on the part of teachers. Involving the learner in the design of the learning process, identifying his or her previous learning experiences and using these in the new learning situation, allowing for individual approaches to, and styles of, learning which may include the use of a variety of resources and materials, will present significant pedagogical challenges to the teacher.

His or her whole rôle will have to alter if the individual needs of the learner are to be met. Didactic teaching methods will have to be replaced by techniques within which the teacher has the function of negotiator and facilitator in the learning process. Such an overall approach will highlight the extra support required by the learner with special needs and this will be taken into account when planning individual learning opportunities.

For many students with special needs practical experiences provide the most appropriate method of learning. This is particularly true where any form of learning difficulty is involved. Tangible experiences which are seen by the student to have relevance to their situation are not merely effective alternative teaching strategies, they are also powerful stimuli which can motivate the student and assist in enhancing their self-confidence. This latter aspect is particularly relevant to those students with special needs who have been sheltered or protected from the reality of the world as it is. However, in order to ensure that the student does learn from his or her experiences, the teacher has to be involved in a careful process of preparation, guidance, support and monitoring.

A variety of practical suggestions regarding how to develop flexible and varied approaches to the management of learning for students with special needs has been made by Dee in 'Strategies for Teaching and Learning', module 4 of *From Coping to Confidence*[15] and by Faraday and Harris in 'Training/Teaching and Learning Strategies', module 5 of *Learning Support*.[16] More general discussions on the main educational/training implications of disabling conditions expressed in terms of special learning needs, together with the practical implications of these to the development of individual educational/training programmes are to be found in: *A College Guide: Meeting Special Educational Needs*[17] and 'The Educational Implications of Disability'.[18]

Providing individual counselling and support

Counselling and guidance are important elements of any programme leading to the acquisition of a vocational qualification. Again, this is something which, at the best, has been taken for granted, or, worse still, has been ignored or considered unnecessary. This element of the education/training process requires just as much attention as any other, especially where students with special needs are concerned, and where such students are to be found in integrated settings working alongside their non-disabled peers.

All counselling and support which is provided for students with special needs should be subject to the following general criteria:

1 The availability of counselling and support facilities should be identified at the outset in any policy/publicity statements issued by the college/training provider.

2 Sensitive methods should be available for students with special needs to identify themselves. This should include the identification of an individual key contact person to whom the student with special needs can relate.

3 Acceptance of students with special needs for a course of training should be undertaken using the same criteria as for any other student. Difficulties which present themselves and which are associated with any form of disability should be fully investigated and solutions sought at this initial stage.

4 Very often the individual student with special needs will be able to identify his or her own support needs. It is important however that any personnel involved in offering counselling services to students with special needs are fully aware of the following points:
   - Problems of access to and within the college;
   - Adapted facilities available within the college;
   - The identification of difficulties likely to occur within the learning situation and ways of overcoming these;
   - Awareness of support agencies both within and outside the college.

The need for counselling and support exists at a number of stages which occur during the lifetime of an education/training programme. These are as follows:

1 Selection/pre-entry (ie, before starting a course);
2 Induction/entry (ie, at the beginning of a course);
3 Experience/during (ie, during a course);
4 Transition/exit and progression (ie, preparing to leave a course).

Processes established to meet the needs of students with special needs will be of relevance and value to all students. Key questions such as: 'Is the programme appropriate to the student's purpose?' and 'Is the programme within the student's capabilities?' will have to be addressed for everyone embarking on a programme leading to the acquisition of an NVQ. What is especially important for those with special needs is that the questions are posed in the first place.

All too often, in the past, inaccurate judgements have been made about the capacity of students with special needs to undertake a programme of vocational training. These judgements have been made on the thinnest of grounds where misinformation and even mythology have ruled the day. Equally, providers of education and training have doubted their own capacities to support students with special needs within the institution. On the other hand it is now widely accepted that, with appropriate support, employment is a possible outcome of education/training for even the most severely disabled students.

The new opportunities afforded by the NVQ framework will go far in helping to remove the barriers encountered by students with special needs.

However, the major problem for providers of education/training is that they are often inexperienced, and therefore afraid, in dealing with students with special needs. This results in invalid judgements being made. Staff are inexperienced also in knowing where to go for help in overcoming problems. Very often the resolution of these difficulties is available close at hand, within the institution. Where this is not possible, then a wide range of support/resource agencies is available nationally.[19]

Finding alternative methods of assessing for competence

In NVQs, units of competence, elements and performance criteria are clearly stated. Traditionally education/training programmes specify learning outcomes for students to meet. Within NVQ-led programmes these targets are already specified within the statement of competence. However, where traditional and often indirect methods of assessment persist, these effectively limit the way in which achievement is demonstrated.

While such learning outcomes are fixed and are therefore unchangeable, there may well however be equally valid but alternative ways in which the student can demonstrate her or his competence to the standards laid down in the performance criteria. Thus, as the NCVQ states in *Assessment in National Vocational Qualifications*[20]: 'The National Council will not specify particular types of assessment to be adopted. A variety of types and methods will be accepted depending on the elements of competence to be assessed.' It also says: 'The mode of assessment should not place unnecessary additional demands which may inhibit or prevent a candidate from showing what they know or understand.' These are important statements of principle in so far as students with special needs are concerned. In the past many people working with students with special needs have felt that vocational programmes have been orientated towards formal and inflexible assessment methods which have unfairly discriminated against such students. This message has been clearly outlined by the NCVQ in *Access and Equal Opportunities in Relation to National Vocational Qualifications*:[21]

> the way in which competence is demonstrated and assessed may vary. Any valid method of assessment which provides evidence that competence has been achieved to the specified standard is permissible. For example, it may be possible to substitute written questions with oral ones, or allow the use of mechanical aids such as typewriters or tape-recorders. Such changes will normally need to be approved by the relevant awarding body, but NVCQ will be encouraging awarding bodies to be flexible in tolerating alternative assessment methods, provided that this does not result in changes in the performance criteria. *The issue is that the mode of assessment should not constitute*

an artificial barrier to gaining an award if performance in respect of that competence is not dependent on the one mode.

In developing alternative methods of assessment, the following points might be considered.

1 In certain situations the assessment method as specified cannot be changed and remain valid. For example, if the requirement is to show how materials might be lifted, handled and stacked safely, then this is a practical assessment and is the only way in which it can be undertaken.

2 Wherever it is possible students should be able to take advantage of developments in new technology which enable them to overcome the limitations imposed by their disability, but only if this enables them to perform to the set criteria. Assessment which is assisted by the use of aids and equipment, or by the exchange of unsuitable equipment for that which can be used by the student, is acceptable. Assistance from another person would have to be limited to those circumstances where the help obtained by the use of that person only enables the student to demonstrate his or her own competence, eg: a scribe for a student with a physical difficulty in writing or an interpreter for a student with a hearing impairment. It would not be acceptable for another person to undertake, on behalf of this student, what is specifically demanded by the performance criteria.

3 Some learning outcomes specify, or at least imply, the use of a particular mode of communication, eg, 'give a ten minute talk . . .'. In these cases the assessment method cannot be changed. However, in many other situations the mode of communication is either unspecified or is irrelevant to the achievement of the learning outcome. In these cases it is acceptable for an alternative method of communication to be used. For example: the use of a tape-recorder or a scribe by a student with a writing difficulty or the presentation of work via the use of a word processor, the use of sign language by students with hearing impairment and the use of large print or braille by students with visual impairments.

Students with special needs have had difficulty, in the past, in gaining access to vocational qualifications and thus employment. Significant advances have been made and the introduction of the NVQ framework should aim to assist and not hinder this process. Barriers should be removed and the process of credit accumulation and the facility of the National Record of Vocational Achievement (NROVA) should further help those with special needs in building up, over a period of time which suits them, a personal profile of abilities and competencies which will also provide for the certification of achievement at levels below full awards via the system of unit credits.

Some specifications of competence, as they are currently written, may disbar some students with special needs. Flexibility needs to be built into the system. The specification of competence and performance criteria should not discriminate against students with special needs without a full examination of procedures and practices together with the fullest exploration of alternative strategies and methods. No one would wish to see the introduction of a separate group of 'special needs qualifications', but if this is not to happen then all of the issues identified above will require attention by all concerned in the design, delivery and the assessment of NVQs.

REFERENCES

1 *Handicapped Youth at Work*, Paris, OECD/CERI, 1985.
2 DES, *Special Educational Needs*. Report of the Committee of Enquiry into the Education of Handicapped Children and Young People (The Warnock Report), Cmnd 7212, London, HMSO, 1978.
3 *Disabled Youth – The Right to Adult Status*, Paris, OECD/CERI, 1988.
4 *International Classification of Impairments, Disabilities and Handicaps*, Geneva, World Health Organisation, 1980.
5 *Access and Equal Opportunities in Relation to National Vocational Qualifications*, NCVQ Information Leaflet No. 3, London, NCVQ, 1988.
6 Ibid.
7 *Education Act*, London, HMSO, 1981.
8 *Education (Special Education Needs) Regulations*, London, HMSO, 1983.
9 *YTS Special Training Needs. A Code of Practice*, Sheffield MSC, 1988.
10 *A College Guide: Meeting Special Educational Needs*, London. FEU/Longmans, 1986.
11 *Descriptions, Definitions and Directions: Special Needs in Further and Continuing Education*. Special Needs Occasional Paper No. 7, London, FEU/Longmans, 1989.
12 *Flexible Learning Opportunities and Special Educational Needs*, London, FEU, 1988.
13 *What It Means For Colleges*. London, NCVQ, 1988.
14 *Learning Support. A Staff Development Resource: pack for those working with learners who have special needs*, London, Training Agency, FEU/SKILL, 1989.
15 *From Coping to Confidence. A Staff Development Resource Pack for FE teachers of students with moderate learning difficulties*, London, DES/FEU, 1985. Video
16 *Learning Support*, op. cit.
17 *A College Guide*, op. cit.

18 J. Male and C. Thomson, *The Educational Implications of Disability*, London, Radar, 1985.
19 D. Hutchinson, 'Co-operation and Co-ordination', in *From Coping to Confidence*, op. cit., Module 7 and S. Faraday and R. Harris, 'Sources of Help and Advice', in *Learning Support*, op. cit., Module 9.
20 *Assessment in National Vocational Qualifications*, NCVQ Information Leaflet No. 4, London, NCVQ, 1988.
21. Op. cit.

9. Occupational competence and work-based learning: the future for Further Education?

Roy Boffy

THE END OF THE QUALIFICATION MONOPOLY

Why do we have a further education system? One motor vehicle apprentice had the answer: 'I've come to get my sitting gills.' The City and Guilds of London Institute is long established in the field of vocational qualifications. The student apprentice knew what game he was in: the paper chase. So far as he was concerned his college course was not about becoming a competent motor mechanic, but about getting a piece of paper to show he was 'qualified'. If we had given it to him at enrolment he probably wouldn't have come back. He was typical of many employed students. The relevance to their everyday working lives of what they were asked to do at college was not clear. Full-time students knew no better. They knew only that 'qualifications' were a passport to a job, and employers continued to use these 'qualifications' as selection mechanisms, even when there was no apparent connection between them and the job that needed doing. 'He's got maths, but he can't even give change!' 'She's got English, but I couldn't trust her to take a telephone message.' Such complaints, well-founded or not, were an inevitable part of the system. It is noticeable that not many employers sent their employees back to college for retraining. This may have something to do with a reluctance to train, it has as much to do with employers' perceptions of colleges as places where young people go to get their certificates before the real job of production starts.[1]

Many in further education would regard this as a parody, at best a distorted description of the bad old days. Things are much better now, they would argue. Syllabuses are more imaginative and less content-besotted than they were; learning is more experiential; teaching more facilitative, less didactic. Colleges are open to a broader client group. Fundamentally, however, the system is not much changed. The innovations tend to be at the margin. Further education is still about providing fixed-duration, linear courses which lead directly to syllabus-based qualifications. Traditionally it aimed to provide education and training for young workers on time-served apprenticeships and to give them some portable evidence to that effect. Its structures and traditions are still largely geared to this provision.

Qualifications were used either to select candidates for entry to the labour market or to certify that a particular course of education had been followed. Their main function was to deny access to those who did not possess them. This was particularly the case with academic qualifications, but even vocational qualifications were about providing a broadly-based technical preparation for entry to the labour market. They were not about recognising competence in the workplace as the basis for their award.

It was, and is, generally recognised that competence is gained after work experience. It can be trained for, but it cannot be achieved pre-entry. These qualifications are not without value though their content is often detached from the world they seek to prepare for. At best they provide a reasonably thorough grounding for the world of work. Above all, though, being pre-entry awards, they were targeted at, and designed for, young people. They have little relevance to the training needs of older workers or their employers – a major growth area for training, given the changes that are taking place in employment and technology. For adult workers, in particular, the key issues are to give recognition to competence in new work rôles as these develop under the pressure of technological and other changes. For young workers, and would-be workers, the issue is more to do with preparing them for work and with giving them a grounding which will enable them to become competent more quickly in their future work rôles.

What is needed is an FE system which aims to develop occupational competence within the whole labour force. This is radically different from a system which is mainly concerned with the initial, pre-entry training of young people about to enter the labour market.

NCVQ is seeking to change this traditional 'credentialism'. NVQs will be 'standards-based', 'relevant', 'comprehensible', 'credible', 'accessible', will 'enable progression', and be 'cost-effective'.[2] Translating the stated aims of NCVQ into practice will take a little while. The much needed qualitative shift in the nature of qualifications which is being promoted by NCVQ will need a longer time scale than is presently envisaged. There is evidence of existing qualifications and skills tests expediently yoked together and being deemed to meet NCVQ criteria even when they do not. There is fudging of the issue of where competence may be demonstrated. We know that current approvals are only 'conditional' but expedients have a habit of becoming permanent structures. One change, however, that NVQs will almost certainly bring about is the separation of the award of a 'certificate of competence' from the location, pace and mode of learning. In other words, further education will lose its virtual monopoly on the award of vocational qualifications.

Theoretically, when a competence-based system of qualifications is in place, it should be possible for any worker to approach an accredited assessor and ask for her or his competence to be judged against the specified criteria for the award of the qualification. So long as the criteria are met, the award will be given. If competence is not demonstrated this indicates a training need. This system places a clear separation between the award, which is simply based on performance regardless of prior experience, and training which may or may not lead to competent performance. The training can be delivered anywhere. The rewards will go to those trainers who most efficiently and effectively help workers to become competent. Separating the award of vocational qualifications from attendance on education and training courses, should enable education and training providers to focus more sharply on what their role actually is – to assist in the improvement of performance at work, not to certificate the outcomes of their own provision as if that were the same thing. Whether or not this system works depends on whether standards and criteria can be developed which truly reflect competence in a dynamic labour market. If this does not happen, the qualifications themeslves will fall into disrepute. The fundamental issues of effective training which helps people to become competent will remain. There is evidence[3] to suggest that, for employed workers at least, employers are more interested in training which results in real improvements in quality and productivity than they are in qualifications as such.

This situation will force the issue of quality in training to the forefront in further education. Colleges would be wrong to assume that all will be well so long as their course-based qualifications have the 'kitemark' of NCVQ. This would be to confuse qualifications with quality, and so persist in all of the deficiencies of the present system, but in a much more open market. If vocational qualifications can be gained without attendance on a college course, why go to college? There will be many other competitors claiming that their training provision is at least as good as that provided in the public sector.

Further education can hope to maintain its position only if it tackles some fundamental training issues which, effectively addressed, result in quality provision. Traditional further education was set up to meet a particular need for long duration training. This worked well so long as this was all it was asked to do. The traditional expertise and delivery system is now increasingly inappropriate given the decline in the youth population, for it has produced a number of characteristics that are now undesirable – it is inflexible; it is too dependent on young people for its client group; it is too concerned with teaching rather than learning, and it is too acquiescent in accepting as holy writ syllabuses handed down by others. Further education thrived on servicing the qualification market. In the sense that student demand for qualifications was met, it could claim to be successful. Yet qualifications are, at best, an analogue for the outcomes of quality training. The future credibility of further education lies in its ability to support the labour market through the provision of quality training. This will require FE to penetrate new markets, particularly in adult retraining, to demonstrate real cost-benefits, and to develop new modes of delivery.

FE AND QUALITY

What, then, constitutes quality in training and how can FE contribute to its development? Effective quality training must address at least three key economic issues:

1 The need for improved work performance, which results in improvements in product quality and design; improved service; improved productivity and reliability; improved information handling; innovation and product development and better marketing.
2 The need for a competent workforce which, at all levels, is capable of carrying out 'work rôles or jobs to the standard required in employment'.[4] NCVQ is aiming to establish a national system of competence-based qualifications. It is, however, necessary to distinguish between training for competence and qualifications which claim to reflect that competence. Many frequently fail to make this distinction when they argue the need for a 'qualified labour force'. To bemoan the fact that only 40 per cent of the British labour force has a recognised qualification, or to claim that German and Japanese economic performance is a direct result of having a highly-qualified labour force misses the point. Competence, not qualification, is the real issue.
3 The need for a workforce capable of managing changes caused by the speed of technological change and the turbulence that this induces in the economy, alongside other changes in working practices and the world market. In practice this means develop-

ing a versatile workforce capable of adapting to new situations. Workers will need to be able to transfer skills to new situations, develop new skills, and upgrade their skill levels. They will need to be more highly motivated and more technically competent. All of these issues were identified in the *New Training Initiative*,[5] which remains a useful policy backstop for those interested in sustaining quality development. This implies new approaches to training, and to training styles and methods which help trainees develop the skills necessary for the management of change, alongside the more job-specific skills which often provide the initial motivation to learn.

Quality training can be recognised by its contribution to these basic economic imperatives: to improved work performance, to the development of competence and to the creation of a more adaptable workforce. There is implicit in this the notion that further education will need to take a broad view of its rôle in supporting the labour market. Further education must develop a curriculum responsible to individual demands and better tailored to labour market requirements. Basing this curriculum on the *whole* work rôle of workers should enable further education to avoid the traps of narrow vocationalism on the one hand and unrelated theorising on the other.

LEARNING AND OCCUPATIONAL COMPETENCE

Making the work rôle the focus for learning is the starting point for the development of occupational competence. It brings into a coherent perspective the whole range of responsibilities carried by workers, the relationships that need to be maintained at work, and into the management skills that need to be exercised. Mansfield and Mathews[6] have proposed a useful framework for the understanding of what constitutes competence within a work rôle. They suggest that there are three interrelated components:

1 The skills required to carry out tasks (task skills);
2 The skills required to manage the relationship between tasks (task management skills);
3 The skills necessary to manage the work environment, including unexpected occurrences (job/rôle environment skills).

They argue that the traditional focus on training for particular task-specific skills ignores important dimensions of occupational competence and does not reflect the complex reality of most work environments. For example, a painter and decorator will carry out a number of tasks in decorating a room. Typically, stripping off paint and wallpaper; cleaning down; hanging wallpaper; applying paint; removing and replacing radiators, and so on. However, the overall efficiency of the operation is highly dependent on the successful management of the relationship between those tasks (we wouldn't think much of a decorator who painted the woodwork before painting the ceiling!), on the attention paid to safe working practices, and on the care taken to avoid damage to fixtures and furniture. In addition, the decorator may well have to work well with other people, to establish good relationships with clients, to negotiate a price for a job, to advise on colour co-ordination, and, especially if self-employed, to manage accounts, plan the work of others, and so on.

It is evident that the range of skills required in work is diverse and encompasses communication, planning, problem-solving and inter-personal skills in addition to task-specific skills. In respect of adaptability and skills transfer, these management skills are precisely those which have applicability in a wide range of working environments, while the task-specific skills usually have relatively limited transfer value. Ironically, it is often the task-specific skills for which we train, while the more generally applicable skills are neglected and unrecognised. To survive as an advanced industrial society, we need to recognise individuals as possessing a whole battery of skills and talents to bring to new situations. Emphasising the full range of skills needed to cope with the work rôle increases the likelihood of this happening, and provides a clear rationale for training which is more than task-specific.

CAN FE RESPOND?

In the traditional model, syllabuses are designed by examining bodies, usually on an expert-led basis of what subject panels think ought to be in the syllabus and usually expressed in terms of subjects or similarly cognate vocational disciplines. These syllabuses are then handed down to teachers who process students through their content and assess student performance in the light of their progress in terms of the syllabus content and implied criteria for success. Students are then examined, results moderated, and certificates awarded. There is little opportunity to modify syllabus content, at least in the short-run, and students' learning needs are defined in terms of the syllabus itself. It is a structure that exists in and for itself and which seeks little external justification for its own internal logic: 'Why are we doing this?' 'Because it's on the syllabus' is an oft-heard exchange.

The hand-me-down curriculum is the one with which most FE

teachers are familiar. It is similar to the academic model pursued in schools and higher education. It has its uses, but it is not useful in terms of preparing young people to work in an environment which requires the synthesis of a whole range of skills and knowledge, or of helping older people to adjust to and manage change. The academic model is analytical and theory-driven. The curriculum model derived from occupational competence is synthesising and experience-based.

Further education has traditionally been preoccupied with teaching, rather than with learning, with inputs rather than with outcomes. Usually, the teaching is to the same group of students, to an unchanging syllabus, at the same time each week for 36 or fewer weeks per year, starting in September and finishing, with the examinations, in June. Minor changes to this routine are accommodated, major changes rarely take root as common practice. It is remarkable how much of FE is still like this. The structures and systems in place all reflect this preoccupation with inputs and with teaching as an activity which is worthwhile in itself. Timetables, class hours, holidays, examination schedules, subjects, registers, rows of desks, teaching aids. Students are rarely mentioned except in the context of student-hours and full-time equivalents – the units of currency, rather than the raison d'être.

To respond fully to the implications of developing occupational competence, further education colleges must develop more responsible structures. Work roles are highly individual – they are subject to constant change as technology, working practices and markets develop. The curriculum, therefore, must be kept under constant review. FE staff need to be continually developing their materials and teaching approaches to keep pace with labour market demands.

The Responsive College Project[7] explored many of the issues associated with flexibility and the management of change in colleges of further education, yet still many colleges see marketing as more to do with selling an existing course than with developing innovative provision.

The fundamental change that has to take place requires a shift in attitudes and perceptions: as a system, FE needs to see itself as a provider of courses. This shift in attitudes and perceptions will have to be followed by changes in behaviour and expectations, both by the managers of the system and the teaching and other staff within it. New structures and controls will be required in order to manage change, as will managerial skills different from those required to administer a stable system. These new structures and controls will need to evolve with time, but elements of them are already there, usually in the more marginalised aspects of current provision, for example, the more flexible modes of delivery associated with team-teaching, assignment work, workshop provision, and student-centred learning packages.

WORK-BASED LEARNING

A productive way forward for FE colleges in their progress towards the delivery of quality vocational education and training provision aimed at developing occupation competence is offered by work-based learning. This has been defined as:

> 'Linking learning to the work role and having three inter-related components, each of which provides an essential contribution to that learning process.
>
> - structuring learning in the workplace;
> - providing appropriate on-job training/learning opportunities;
> - identifying and providing relevant off-job learning opportunities.'[8]

Identification of learning requirements

The starting point in any learning process is the identification of learning needs. In work based learning, for example, these learning needs relate to the work rôles people are expected to perform (these can be expressed in the format of NVQ units). Once these needs are identified, training programmes can be designed specifically to meet them.

The analysis of training needs is a two-way process. An analysis of the full range of skills and knowledge needed by competent workers is necessary to set targets for development. An analysis of the existing skills and knowledge of learners is necessary to establish the starting point for development. It is the gap between the desired outcome and the starting point - the learning gap - that has to be crossed with the assistance of the trainer. This analytical process is considerably assisted if the analyst uses a framework designed for the purpose.

The core skills[9] developed by MSC in the context of YTS but having an application throughout vocational education and training, are a useful tool in the delivery and assessment of work-based learning. They provide an analytical framework and a common language to assist in the full identification of the range of skills needed in the work rôle. These skills, broadly number, communication, problem-solving and practical - are defined by their commonness to a wide range of tasks and activities and are claimed to be essential to successful performance in them. They tend to stress the similarity between experiences, rather than the differences between them; to highlight opportunities for transfer and the relevance of previous experience, and to assist in the identification of learning needs. This is particularly important in retraining workers for new jobs. The job-and-task-specific skills are often relatively easy to train for once the broad similarities between jobs are recognised and built upon.

The diagnostic and formative assessment of work-based learning is about identifying needs in this context and so sets training objectives. Curriculum development is the whole process of designing appropriate customised learning experiences, implementing them, monitoring them in order to assess their effectiveness in the light of the desired objectives, and modifying them in the light of this evaluation.

Experience suggests that most people learn most effectively when they are exposed to learning experiences that mirror the synthesised nature of their daily lives, when they are given the opportunity to reflect on those experiences and to derive theories, or generalisations, from them as a guide to future action and understanding. It does not, of course, follow from this that individual needs must be met on an individual, one-to-one, basis, in isolation from other learners. Indeed, some learning needs can only be met in group situations – it is difficult to conceive of interpersonal skills being developed without involving other people.

Work-based learning does not prescribe a particular learning method. A whole variety of learning approaches may be used as appropriate. What is important is to identify learning needs within the work rôle and then to design appropriate training programmes to meet them, taking account of individual styles and preferences. For example, a learning need may arise because of new legislation. One learner may prefer to find out about this from a journal and to think through its implications alone. Another may prefer to attend a lecture and feed back the information through discussion with colleagues. Yet another may prefer to attend a seminar which offers the opportunity for in-depth review of the likely effects with an expert group leader. This attention to individual learning needs, derived from the individuality of work rôles, is a major strength of work-based learning. It ensures that training is relevant to the individual and is perceived as such.

The consequences of failing to address individual learning needs are easy enough to identify. How many teachers have attended in-service training events in the last couple of years and have come back indignant at 'time-wasting' and 'irrelevance'? How many teachers have taken the lesson to heart and applied it to their own provision for students? Many teachers reject didactic modes of delivery, yet continue to apply them to their own students. They do not learn easily from their own experiences. It is precisely because training so often fails to meet real needs that it is held in such low esteem and treated as a cost rather than an investment.

Work-based learning then, starts with the question of what a person needs to be able to do in order to perform effectively in the work rôle. Formative assessment to determine learning needs is about helping people to learn more effectively. It is the starting point for an iterative learning cycle which was fully explored in the FEU paper *Experience, Reflection, Learning.*[10] It creates a situation for FE staff analogous to that of a sports coach. The coach will analyse the training needs of the players, will provide a training programme aimed at meeting those needs, often with plenty of match practice thrown in, but at the end of the day the players will go on to the field and it is there that their competence will be judged. The better the assessment of needs and the more accurately the training is designed to meet those needs, then the more likelihood there is of a competent performance resulting. There is still a gap, though, between training and actual performance. The effectiveness of the training will be judged in the light of that performance, not in the light of the training itself.

The delivery of work-based learning

A curriculum in FE that supports learner-centred work-based learning will be much more in the control of the providers of vocational education than was the traditional FE curriculum. It should offer certain guarantees that the whole range of skills necessary to successful functioning in work rôles is being developed, as well as the opportunity to develop skills and knowledge particular to a given occupation. It will require structures which enable the learning needs of individuals to be met on an individual or collective basis. It will need to be flexible and dynamic. The content of this new curriculum will need to emphasise the development of transferable skills within the context of developing more job-specific skills and knowledge. The work that people are doing, or wish to do, provides a prime motivator in vocational education.

Project- or assignment-based approaches are often appropriate to providing the curriculum structures required in work-based learning.[11] It is easier for teachers to respond to individual learning needs within the relatively large-scale structures offered by project-based activities than within more conventional teaching situations; students have more responsibility for their own learning; it is possible to develop a broad range of overtly relevant skills, and to carry them out on an individual or group basis.

Such approaches are not the only ones appropriate to work-based learning, however. Workshop approaches, where students have access to a range of learning resourses geared to meeting individual needs, are often used to good effect, as are other more free-standing open- and distance-learning materials, simulations, games and rôle-plays. The test is whether the approaches are helping the learners to learn effectively. Whether or not students develop the transferable skills critical to the successful performance of work rôles is dependent on the way teachers approach their teaching. More active, student-centred approaches such as projects, assignment, rôle-plays, simulations and tutorials, are more likely to develop a range of problem-solving and communication skills, for example, than are more traditional didac- tic, teacher-centred approaches.[12]

A further characteristic of work-based learning of particular relevance to FE is that it promotes integration between the various locations in which learning linked to the work rôle may occur. While the workplace itself clearly has major advantages as a location for learning (even if, at present, the learning that occurs at work is largely unrecognised) and is, arguably, the only place in which an assessment of competence can take place with any validity, it also has its drawbacks. The pressures of production or of customer demands, for example, militate against skill development or the acquisition of new skills. Planned on-job training can overcome some of these drawbacks and provide staff with direct experience of equipment or procedures that they will use in their everyday work, but this is restricted to company-specific systems and, unless carefully managed, offers little opportunity for transfer – indeed commercial pressures may actively work against this broader labour market need. Off-job training has considerable potential: it provides an environment away from the direct pressures of the workplace, where learning needs can take priority over other concerns.

Curriculum content and process in off-the-job education and training is more obviously under the direct control of FE than is the content and process in the other two dimensions of work-based learning: the workplace itself and on-job training situations. It offers the opportunity to learn new skills in a relatively stress-free situation; it provides the opportunity for reflection upon experience, for guidance, counselling and personal support; it allows students to learn to use complex or dangerous equipment in a safe and protected environment; it allows theorising and generalisation to be drawn from and grounded in experience; it can readily act as a stimulus to new ideas and creative thinking; it can help students to make connections between apparently disconnected experiences and to learn from them; it can facilitate reviewing of progress and the setting of new targets.

Unfortunately, this potential is rarely realised in practice. Much off-job training, for young people and older workers, is more dominated by teaching than it is by learning; it is often fragmentary in itself, with the day being divided up into 'subjects'; its content is often out-of-date, ill-informed and sometimes simply wrong; 'theory' is divorced from 'practice'. This is made all the more irksome when it is the only part of the whole learning/training process which attracts formal, accredited, recognition.

In summary, then, work-based learning contributes to the development of high quality vocational education and training programmes by:

- raising awareness of the full range of skills needed for occupational competence;
- focusing on the learning needs of individual workers;
- promoting integration within training programmes.

ASSESSMENT OF OCCUPATIONAL COMPETENCE

The function of the assessment of competence developed in the workplace is to weigh the evidence of the achievement of competences against explicit performance criteria. The demonstration of competence to the standards set is evidence that learning has been effective.

A competence-based system of qualifications, with clear standards and criteria such as is proposed by NCVQ, should go some way to alleviating the dangers inherent in any system of work-based assessment. But we should not underestimate the difficulties involved. First, there is the problem of specifying the richness and complexity of human achievement that constitutes competence in a work rôle so that it is possible to assess when that point has been reached. Traditionally assessment has tended to be based on what is relatively easy to measure and to replicate. It is this narrow focus on the measurable which has often caused so much distortion in the curriculum, and led to so many frustrations with the outcomes of education and training. The resultant models of assessment for certification are themselves lacking refinement and subtlety, but the fact that they have been the only models tends constantly to corrupt the process of developing more reliable forms of assessment.

The assessment of the outcomes of work-based learning will look very different from traditional assessment. It will, for example, contain much more information from more sources and be more contextualised than is traditionally the case. There will be no marks, grades or profile statements, no 'top of the class', no single-subject titles. There is potentially a mass of information to be generated about performance, for the assessment of work-based learning generates a much richer tapestry of individual skills and abilities than do traditional paper-based assessments. Obtaining and managing this information will require new skills and a wider range of assessment techniques and instruments than we have used to date. It will also require the users of assessments to develop skills in interpreting the information generated. For example, in selection of employment, selectors will need to match information about performance to the requirements of the job on offer. This is, no doubt, a more difficult process than simply relying on examination results to do the job of selection, or relying on the gut reaction of interviewers. However, it should result in more effective selection.

The difficulties in the assessment of the outcomes of work-based learning, then, are considerable. They relate principally to the issues of making judgements about performance to agreed standards, to specifying these standards and the associated criteria, to describing achievement and relating this to the specified standards, to summarising this for the purposes of certification, and to interpreting the information provided.[13] Some of these issues can be resolved by a recognition that many of our assessments only need be good enough to fulfil particular purposes – suitability for employment, or for further training, or for access to higher education courses, for instance – and do not need to be rigorous in the sense that, for example, psychometric tests are rigorous. Perfection in the assessment of competence is probably unattainable, and would certainly be extremely expensive, given the variety of human behaviour and the contexts in which it is exhibited. In chasing the chimera of objectivity and reliability we tend to neglect much valuable assessment information and generate many distortions in the process. What we need is a rounded picture of achievement from which we may draw reasonable conclusions about potential.

Some of these technical problems may take a little while to resolve to the point where it is possible for an individual to seek full accreditation of competence on demand. Whether or not they are resolved in a way which hinders or helps the development of relevant education and training provision depends on NCVQ's criteria for approval. One of the major concerns with NVQs at present is that conditional accreditations are running well ahead of the technical work that needs to be done to support them.[14]

NEW SKILLS FOR FE TEACHERS

Work-based learning and competence-based qualifications make teachers think more clearly about what students need to learn to prepare them for their work rôles, and how they can most effectively help students to reach these objectives. Work-based learning will require FE teachers to develop a whole battery of new skills, which in themselves should lead to heightened professionalism and greater job satisfaction. They will need to develop and use a much broader range of teaching and assessment techniques. Many traditional techniques will, of course, remain useful as diagnostic tools – skill tests, for example, and even standard knowledge tests where this is a significant part of the job being trained for. Much more emphasis, though, will need to be placed on analytical and observational techniques, on negotiating with learners, on helping people develop curriculum vitae, on helping people identify the range of skills they possess already and suggesting ways in which they can further develop, and on counselling and guidance skills. These techniques, already well-developed in parts of the education service (in special needs education for example), need to become part of the professional tool kit of all teachers in further education.

Similarly, teachers need to develop closer relationships with employers and to become more familiar with the range of skills deployed in occupations. They will need access to the workplace and to gain the confidence of managers and shop floor staff if they are to observe actual working practices and so enable the identification of the full range of skills that workers deploy in their work rôles, which can be used to facilitate curriculum development. Once confidence and trust have been established, employers may be more willing to invite staff to advise on, and intervene in, in-company training programmes and processes; FE staff can help to demonstrate the need for training and develop programmes where none exist.[15] As and when the separation of qualifications from courses, as heralded by NCVQ, comes about, FE staff could well develop new roles as validators of competent performance. This will be much easier to acheive if credibility has been developed beforehand. In addition, developing close links with employers should make it easier to demonstrate a measurable pay-off from training, in terms of reduced labour turnover, reduced complaints or rejects, and improved quality and productivity. This should help convince sceptical employers of the economic value of training. In general, staff need to get involved in the whole curriculum for work-based learning, developing new skills as training consultants and brokers. They may be instrumental in persuading employers towards a view of training which has more to do with long-term survival and adaptability in the face of endemic change. The quality of the process needs to be demonstrated by outcomes in the market place – a connection which few education institutions have yet been able to establish with any degree of conviction.

Work-based learning, with its focus on the work rôle, links broad social and educational values to effective work performance and provides a strong rationale for progressive developmental approaches to training. By sustaining a focus on learning needs within a work rôle, work-based learning acts to sustain a unity of purpose throughout the learning programme and provides a constant reference point to check the relevance of any part of that programme.

THE FUTURE RESTS ON QUALITY

Further Education colleges have apparently changed more than most institutions over the last 60 years. They have gone from being night schools and Mechanics' Institutes in the 1930s, through the period of rapid growth of part-time day release caused by the economic boom of post-war reconstruction in the 1950s and 1960s, through the steady growth in full-time courses in the 1970s and the rapid growth in demand generated by youth unemployment in the 1980s. Yet this appearance of change masks a reality of resistance: they have accommodated change rather than responded to it, bringing innovations into line or bolting them on and then discarding them once the immediate pressure was removed. The instances of this are many: a few examples will serve to make the point. *Better Opportunities in Technical Education*[16] looked for a broader curriculum for technical apprentices. Further Education bolted on English and General Studies, and then unbolted it, leaving the basic problem unresolved. The Technician Education Council[17] sought a modularised unit accreditation package: its awards were soon straightjacketed into courses and classes. Unified Vocational Preparation[18] looked for purpose-built packages, often got them, and then was subsumed into YTS and vanished. YOP[19] looked for student-centred, roll-on roll-off provision and suffered the same fate as UVP. Where they still exist 48-week extended-year ITB-sponsored programmes have largely reverted to 36 and 38 weeks.

There are, however, causes for optimism. First, positive people exist. There is a growing number of senior managers – Principals and other senior staff in colleges – who are not particularly interested in simply sustaining the status quo and who see clear threats to the survival of an unreformed FE system. There is a growing number of teaching staff in colleges, often with a background in what used to be called 'the new FE'. They are excited, rather than threatened, by the changes in prospect. They have a clear student-centred ideology, and see much great professional and personal satisfaction in developing new skills and approaches. There is much greater contact with industry. Teaching staff, via the mechanisms of PICKUP,[20] in-service secondments, and market research remits, are more often out in industry and working with companies to identify and meet training needs. Many LEAs are using grants imaginatively to promote this greater collaboration and there is evidence that teachers are responding and enjoying the process.

In my own Authority (Dudley), there has been a concerted collaborative effort between the LEA and its colleges to persuade lecturers to engage in a constructive dialogue with local industry. The strategy has been consistent, and teaching staff have responded positively: 'It was most enjoyable working in local industry, getting back to the hub of things. I enjoy the flexibility, one minute developing and implementing courses in one company, then in another, feeling that I'm not playing a game, but being a part of that company's future in training.'[21] It is interesting that staff, as well as students, recognise that in traditional FE they are really playing a game and that the real world is much more interesting and fruitful.

Then, there are political changes, potentially the most significant of which is the impact of the Education Reform Act on further education. This should give college managers greater freedom to sponsor innovation, while the projected decline in public funding of colleges provides strong incentives to go for high quality training. The rise of private training providers will be a further spur, especially if NVQs are clearly independent of the mode of provision and further education can no longer remain complacent as a monopoly supplier of vocational qualifications. There are other pressures and factors – Training and Enterprise Councils, and 1992, for instance. Taken together they represent a more significant shift in the scenario of education and training than has faced FE in its 100-year history. Maybe the quantitative shift has now become big enough to support and provoke the qualitative leap.

Further education will need to adapt new educational technologies to survive into the twenty-first century. Some colleges already have in place many of the key elements of innovation to allow them to survive: these elements need pulling into a critical mass for change by strong commitment and action from college managers, innovative staff, and LEAs. Further education has a clear rôle to play in the delivery of training within a competence-based system, but as a provider of high quality training rather than as a provider of qualifications. Work-based learning provides a cogent framework for its development.

Expertise in the analysis of training needs, the development of learning programmes, and the assessment of competence will give FE a competitive edge in an increasingly competitive environment. Further education will make or break its reputation in supporting the labour market: what happens to qualifications is subordinate to this. The basic quality issues remain: the need for a versatile, adaptable, technically competent labour force. Further education needs to maintain its integrity in addressing these quality issues, and not to be seduced into the belief that it can carry on much as before.

REFERENCES

1 G Doherty and E Woodhall, *Engineering in a Changing Environment* for Dudley Metropolitan Borough Education Services, 1987.

2 T M Oates, *RVQ in England and Wales: an extraction and collation of the criteria for development*, FESC, IB 2266, 1987.

3 Doherty and Woodhall, op. cit.

4 *National Vocational Qualifications: Criteria and Procedures*, NCVQ, 1989.

5 *The New Training Initiative*, MSC, 1981. Identified the need for the reform of initial skills training, to provide continuing education and training for all school leavers, and to improve training for adults.

6 R Mansfield and D Mathews, *Job Competence: a description for use in vocational education and training*, FESC 1985. The initial framework outlined in this paper has been further developed in *Developments of Assessable Standards for National Certification*, Guidance Notes 2, *Developing Standards by Reference to Functions*, Department of Employment Training Agency, DA52, 1989.

7 The Responsive College Project was funded by MSC and managed by FESC. It ran from 1986 to 1988 and resulted in a major guide to the marketing approach for Colleges: E Theodossin, *The Responsive College*, FESC, 1989.

8 M Levy, *The Core Skills Project and Work-based Learning*, MSC/FESC (IFSL 37), 1987.

9 Levy, op cit. See also *Core Skills in YTS Part One*, MSC 151 1984.

10 *Experience, Reflection, Learning* FEU, 1978. The paper was written to support curriculum development in the Unified Vocational Preparation programme (see below).

11 See *Work-based Projects in YTS* MSC L55, 1985, and the series of exemplar work-based projects published by FESC, for a full description and illustration of the potential of projects to support learning linked to the work rôle.

12 See P Bailey, R Boffy and R Valentine, *Participative Learning and YTS Core*

Skills, FESC IB 2088, 1985, for a fuller discussion of this issue, and also R Boffy, 'Vocational Skills Misunderstood' letter in *The Times Educational Supplement*, 14.3.86, for further discussion on the relationship between 'academic' and 'vocational' education.

13 See, for example, D Mathews, *Assessment in the Workplace*, FESC IB 2219, 1986, for a lucid exposition of the issues involved.

14 See A Wolf, 'Sidestepping the Difficult Issues', in *Competence and Assessment No. 4*, Department of Employment, Training Agency.

15 See L Knight, *A Bucket of Nuts* (provisional title) FEU RP 497 (forthcoming), FEU and Dudley Metropolitan Borough Education Services, for some interesting local case studies of this.

16 *Better Opportunities in Technical Education*, Ministry of Education, 1956. The subsequent Circular 323 advocated liberalising the technical curriculum in a number of ways – the one most commonly adopted was to insert a new subject into the timetable.

17 The Technician Education Council was formed in 1974 with the brief of reforming qualifications for technician-level occupations. Although radical in intent, few colleges restructured their delivery systems to meet the new curriculum, preferring to slot the new demands into established structures.

18 The Unified Vocational Preparation Programme was introduced in 1976 as a joint venture by MSC and the DES. It aimed to provide further education and training for young workers who were not traditionally involved in this. It, rather than YOP, provided the design prototype for YTS. What went wrong thereafter could be the subject of another book.

19 The Youth Opportunities Programme was introduced by MSC in 1978 as part of the government's response to rising youth unemployment. Some interesting innovative provision resulted, especially in the development of social and life skills.

20 The Professional, Industrial and Commercial Updating Programme (PICKUP) was introduced by the DES in 1982 and provides funds to encourage Colleges to undertake training and retraining for employed adults.

21 Knight, op.cit.

10. Accreditation of Prior Learning: The foundation stone of NVQ delivery

John Newman and Nick Llewellin

INTRODUCTION

While most workers in the UK do not hold any vocational qualifications, many achieve competence during their experience at work and throughout life. Within NVQs, the accreditation of prior learning (APL) prepares unqualified adults to claim fair credits for these achievements. By showing the relevance of NVQs to employment, APL provides a means of demystifying qualifications: it provides a non-threatening means of assessment that will encourage greater participation and continued learning.

In some ways the acceptance of APL as a mainstream route to qualifications depends on the successful implementation of NVQs themselves. In the competence-based system of NVQs, where emphasis is placed on the direct assessment of performance rather than on examinations or test based systems, the relevance and importance of evidence of individuals' achievement in the past becomes more apparent than it has been hitherto. With NVQs it is the qualification rather than the method of learning or assessment that is of greater importance. Those credits gained via APL are thus of equal value to those achieved via more traditional routes of assessment. APL must be as rigorous and as reliable as other methods of assessment: it is not to be seen as a soft option.

The APL process begins with the student producing a curriculum vitae and then being helped by a counselling tutor to identify all previous relevant achievements. These achievements may result in part or whole certification towards the full nationally recognised vocational qualification. Most UK adult students will specify gaining a qualification as their main objective in taking part in APL.

To ensure validity, these APL claims must be independently checked by a second approved tutor or assessor, using the elements of competence and associated performance criteria determined by the appropriate validating body (eg C & G, BTEC, RSA). Practical tests, authenticated artefacts, written evidence from past or present employers, simulated work-based assignments, and current workplace testing, are all acceptable ways of identifying the 'can-do' competences that individuals have wholly or partially achieved.

Once an individual's fully-held competences have been identified and credited via APL, a shortened, customised, individual 'topping-up' programme can be designed to develop and then assess the remaining competences necessary to complete the full vocational qualification. These topping-up programmes will require considerable flexibility because each student's assessed-APL starting base is likely to be different.

To retain student confidence and motivation, responsive providers of topping-up tuition will need to integrate the modes and systems of learning that APL students have used informally in the past into economically viable provision. Flexible delivery should include self-paced learning programmes negotiated with each individual student, and a choice of attendance modes for students, including distance learning and assessment based on the student's current work outside the college.

USA AND UK PRACTICE COMPARED

In the USA, APL has long been an established method of opening up access to academic and vocational courses for unqualified adults with useful life or work experience. However, the recognised national validating bodies that dominate UK intermediate vocational education do not have similar counterparts in America. In the USA certificated qualifications are designed and awarded by the individual local community colleges that progress students towards the requirements of academic and vocational provision. This results in much more variation in local college standards than occurs between FE colleges in the UK, all of which are bound by the requirements of national awarding bodies, whose NVQs are based on the national standards set by industry.

Increased college autonomy in the USA allows the use of APL to award individual students general levels of college-certificated qualifications by assessing life-experience portfolios related to whatever total work experience and non-work based living skills they possess. This process leads to standards that can vary considerably at intermediate level between USA college certificates, but results in a much higher take-up rate of Higher Education by adults than in the UK.

The USA community college model is most closely mirrored in the UK by several growing Open Learning Federations of public and voluntary sector providers that progress mature students towards eventual access to HE institutions. Large schemes in Lancashire, London, and Greater Manchester are mainly geared to encouraging disadvantaged adults to gain access to UK academic qualifications via locally designed and validated basic education, including life-experience APL, certificated and assessed independently by each Local Federation.

Even if it were desirable, however, it would be virtually impossible to introduce nationwide the American model of APL-based locally validated college certification in place of the established (and very complicated) structure of UK mainstream vocational qualifications. This is because the UK validating bodies, many of which have developed over more than a century under charter, already give established credibility to their vocational qualifications. These qualifications are recognised as worthwhile and saleable by large numbers of students and employers in the UK and overseas.

NVQs AND APL

The NCVQ was not set up to replace established validating institutions, but to guide the reform and rationalisation of qualifications within clearly defined levels based on nationally defined employer-led competence standards in each vocational area. This should result in a simplified NVQ framework, more accessible to students, more easily understandable to all, and commanding increased confidence from employers. As the NVQ framework is added to, the resulting NVQs will provide the ideal development environment for the APL-based delivery system. NVQ status is given to vocational qualifications that are broken down into separate units containing standards of competence as defined nationally by employers. These awards also allow access to assessment without unnecessary age, experience, entry or learning route restrictions.

The USA community college total-life-experience-portfolio is an acceptable general base for college-validated APL accreditation towards general entry into American HE. The same general APL-based system is equally relevant for UK Open Learning Networks to encourage disadvantaged potential HE access students by accrediting whatever life skills they own. An academic institution will be less

concerned with specific competences than with the general development potential of the individual student at entry to HE.

The APL process in the context of NVQs will only earn employer
credence if it results in students who are competent in occupational
performance. Only the student's prior learning that is relevant to the
vocational competences required in his or her chosen NVQ can be
accredited. Most accreditable prior learning will have been acquired
at the workplace; but hobbies, community activities and running
households also often provide relevant vocational competencies.
These are, however, often difficult to assess.

NVQs have been designed for access by a variety of learning and
assessment routes. With APL, a typed or screened list of the
competence requirements and performance standards that form an
NVQ provides a ready-made initial target for the student and
counsellor. The target is clearly defined, making the task of drawing
up an objective post-APL topping-up learning programme easier for
tutors. The absence of unnecessary entry restrictions means that all
applicants with relevant experience can be accepted. Each individual
can be progressed using flexible methods agreed between students and
tutors without time constraints, but rigorous assessment must be based
on objective proof of competent performance.

NROVA AND THE NCVQ DATABASE

The NCVQ introduced a credit accumulation system in June 1988
based on each student having a NROVA – National Record of
Vocational Achievement. The NROVA is made up of different
sections that correspond to different steps in the learning cycle. It
contains an Action Plan where the individuals' training targets are
outlined, an Assessment Record where their progress towards these
targets is recorded, and sections for certificates relating to the credits
(or units) and NVQs they have achieved. Until the NVQ framework
is completed, achievements in other national vocational awards can
also be included in NROVA.

NROVA is widely available to individuals currently on
Employment Training and the YTS. As more NVQs become
available, the NROVA will be promoted increasingly to those in
employment and other vocational education and training courses.

The NCVQ is committed to open public access to its new database
for NVQs from 1990. The purpose of this database is to outline the
competences required for each NVQ and initially to give details of
other national awards and standards development work.

The extended use of NROVA, and the availability of the NCVQ

database will offer enormous potential for developing APL-based delivery. NROVA will show what an individual has achieved, including achievements gained through experience assessed at the workplace, and the database will provide the details of the NVQ being sought. The database and the NROVA will thus work together to provide a clear picture of the individual's targets and achievements in a national system.

The full implementation of the national system for credit accumulation will take place after the framework of NVQs is completed. At present the potential of the credit accumulation system is clearly hampered by the lack of qualifications available in unit form. Because of its structure, NROVA already offers considerable scope for flexible systems of delivery, including APL. The challenge is to encourage those with employment skills to come forward and get them assessed and accredited within their own individual NROVA. In order to do this we must first make sure that individuals know such a service exists and that their skills may have value in the system.

BENEFITS FOR STUDENTS AND EMPLOYERS

The benefits of APL-based delivery for students are clear. APL gives mature students fair credit for competence that they have acquired at the workplace and in life. APL also gives students real encouragement to progress from that proven base towards the full nationally-recognised qualification that can facilitate career progression and have value in the employment market.

Employers, however, are more ambivalent about qualifications. On the one hand, some have reservations about the whole notion of encouraging staff to gain qualifications and are unsure whether increased access to qualifications via APL will lead to increased labour mobility and wage competition for skilled labour between employers. On the other hand, progressive companies regard investment in qualifications as having benefits that extend beyond the individuals themselves. A company that qualifies its staff is one that is holding up a positive image to its customers, its staff and its investors: it is also a company that people are more likely to want to join than to leave!

THE CHALLENGES FOR FE

The pace of change in FE has quickened significantly during the past ten years, and virtually all college staff have already made the change from being classroom lecturers to managers of learning – albeit with occasional partly-justified groans about the new levels of administrative paperwork! Learning environments and delivery techniques are much more flexible now, with BTEC, and in latter years the YTS, leading the way in creating student counselling and course monitoring structures that require FE staff to make students more aware of their own learning targets, and to become more involved in negotiating individually-paced and achievable learning programmes.

However, the changes of the past ten years will be dwarfed by those that FE colleges must achieve during the next five years. The nationally projected 30 per cent fall in the 16 to 19 population will become reality, leading to greatly increased competition for 16 to 19-year-olds from schools, private sector training organisations, and from industry. This increased competition may lead to reductions in traditional full-time FE college 16 to 19-year-old student intakes well in excess of the general 30 per cent population-group decline.

The potential benefits of APL-based delivery for FE college providers are very clear. FE needs to deliver an alternative system especially designed to meet the individual assessment needs of vocationally experienced adults. FE will also need to offer flexible learning opportunities for those adults who wish to top up their achievements in order to achieve further credits or full qualifications. These factors are compounded by the effects of current demographic trends.

FE college budgets by 1994, as a requirement of the Education Reform Act (ERA), will be totally determined via formulae directly related to annual recruitment expressed in full-time equivalent students. Inevitable reductions in full-time 16 to 19-year-old students, who usually form at least 50 per cent of a typical college's total teaching commitment, will result in colleges actively seeking to preserve budgets and staffing levels by recruiting more part-time employed students and more unemployed and unwaged students. Colleges must replace lost full-time students or risk insolvency and eventual closure under the new funding arrangements. It has been estimated, by the consultants responsible for setting up the new financial arrangements for FE colleges, that there will be 100 fewer colleges in the UK by the mid-1990s.

The quantitative changes of 16 to 19 demography, 16 to 19 labour market competition and tighter post-ERA financial control are already forcing FE colleges to seek greatly increased adult student recruitment for pragmatic reasons of future survival. The increasing rate of technological change and the concomitant changes in industrial practices also combine in a need to train and retrain adults. The FE response to these quantitative factors will be a major drive for mature student recruitment over the next five years. This recruitment drive will target those already in employment and unwaged adult groups with a very wide variety of needs, ranging from basic literacy/numeracy to refresher and updating needs at all levels. Many of these new customers may require complete career path changes, but from an earned base of fair credit for past vocational achievements. NVQs are ideally suited to the individual requirements of the extended adult student market that FE colleges must now exploit. The flexible delivery systems that implementation of NVQs requires involve qualitative changes that match the needs of this new market.

Provision for older students is already regarded in most progressive colleges as a mainstream activity. FE has already started to meet the challenge of raising mature student take-up of college provision as well as improving retention and progression rates. Extra adult provision is currently being implemented on a significant scale in most colleges.

The latest FE drive into comprehensive mature student recruitment must however be much more than a numbers game. In order to attract new, often insecure (and highly discerning!) adult customers, colleges must be made more welcoming and less daunting places. Many colleges are also organising outreach support to attract and reassure local community groups. Equally important, FE must gear the delivery of its provision to fit more flexibly the counselled needs and wants of adults on an individual basis.

APL provides a means of meeting this need and the major UK validating bodies are encouraging the implementation of APL-based delivery (within distant but acceptable timescales). College staff attitudes to APL and NVQ delivery are on the whole positive, and the new type and range of adult customer required for APL within NVQs is exactly what colleges are seeking. NCVQ itself directly sponsors the development of APL delivery techniques as part of its commitment to widening access to qualifications and encouraging the assessment of performance.

The final ingredient necessary for the implementation of APL in FE mainstream provision is an affordable charge for the service to the student. The cost to the student must not exceed normal LEA tuition rates or the access of poorer students to APL will be severely limited.

Sound individual counselling of students is essential for effective APL delivery but may be resource-intensive in terms of requiring one-to-one staff counselling time during the APL process. Staff delivery of subsequent open learning top-up training towards a full NVQ must also be based on individual tuition and small-group learning workshops. Computers will be essential to standardise and therefore cheapen the APL counselling process by using screen-prompt questions to draw out student competences to be credited towards NVQs. The NVQ database will be invaluable in this process.

It will certainly be very much easier to computerise the collation of the students' APL portfolio claims and assess the claims against the relevant NVQ elements of competence and performance criteria, than to computerise the delivery of the remaining top-up training towards the full NVQ. A further challenge will be to track the progress of APL candidates and to include the systematic evaluation of the students' post-APL learning top-up programmes within the range of assessment methods. However, with the use of computer-aided APL counselling, and subsequent delivery of post-APL learning top-up programmes to students in FE college-based open learning workshops, it is estimated that APL can fit students' pockets while satisfying the forthcoming post-ERA funding constraints.

MARKETING APL

A major national campaign to raise awareness of the advantages of prior learning accreditation to individual students is needed to give local providers an established base of initial student interest to recruit from. The unwieldy title of the 'Accreditation of Prior Learning' (APL) will not help these marketing processes but a further change of title at this stage would be a net disadvantage.

Considerable national interest in the area of competence-based training and APL has been expressed by employers. Many new preferred industrial training schemes follow a competence framework. There is also potential for using the procedure of APL within company training. The training programmes can be specified in competence format and a worker's current level of skill can be assessed by a line manager or training supervisor. From this an individual training route can be devised to bring people up to the required level. The implications within organisations for updating and progressive training are considerable. As in-company training begins to use APL techniques, supervisors can be trained in accrediting specific competences and the process of proving skill acquisition becomes much simpler. Marketing APL to employers needs to emphasise these benefits.

The APL approach, with its ability to credit competence is admirably suited to the ET scheme. In marketing APL to ET training agents and managers, it is important the implications of APL are addressed during the initial action plan design carried out by the training agent. This would inevitably mean that the time spent developing the action plan would have to be greater but the resulting product would be an individually tailored learning route that capitalised on past experience and set out a series of realistic goals. It would almost certainly mean that the training manager's role in assessing ET entrants would become simpler and more objective.

Within ET many of the challenges of APL can be overcome, given that scheme assessors are aware of the potential of APL as a method of collecting assessment evidence. For example, programme design could allow evidence to be gained during work placements that would back up the claims within partly assessed student APL portfolios.

NEWPORT/CROSSKEYs APL PROJECT

Background

The Crosskeys and Newport Accreditation of Prior Learning Project formed part of a major national feasibility study commissioned by the Training Agency and managed by NCVQ. The project also has support from Replan, reflecting a concern with training opportunities for the unemployed, and from IBM UK Trust, the charity arm of IBM (in the form of 16 PS2 computers and four printers). The total sponsorship amounts to £100,000.

The initial project was for two years from January 1988, with a twofold brief:

1 To develop APL procedures, enabling adults to claim credit for relevant previous experience (gained within and outside work). This process could lead to a full or part award of either a City and Guilds/Caterbase or BTEC qualification.
2 To set up a prototype of a computer management system, to reduce the cost of APL-based delivery.

The initial qualifications on offer were:

- City and Guilds 705 Catering (and Caterbase)
- City and Guilds 383 Motor Vehicle Engineering
- City and Guilds 201 General Engineering
- BTEC National General Engineering
- BTEC National Business Studies (added in 1989).

Because of the timing of this project, certain work was necessary to construct a temporary NVQ model of qualifications within which to pilot APL in advance of final standards being devised by national LIBs. The project team was thus initially involved in working with the Training Agency and the awarding bodies to convert the existing qualifications into elements of competence with associated performance criteria that would form nationally consistent assessment standards. This was a considerable task. It took place alongside a programme of staff and system development, devised with a great deal of support from Margaret Purdey, the Replan Field Officer for Wales, and the National NCVQ APL project consultant, Susan Simosko.

These standards were completed by the autumn of 1988 and the project was officially launched by the Minister of State for Wales, Mr Wyn Roberts, on 3 November. He saw it as 'a unique breakthrough in helping to fulfil an increasing demand for adults with recognised skills.' This would 'provide new routes to further training and education which will, in turn, open up greater employment opportunities for all who wish to become involved.'

APL in operation

The Crosskeys and Newport APL facility has been designed to provide a supportive, flexible and yet rigorous system for individuals to examine their work and life experiences and to claim credit for the vocational skills and competences they feel they have acquired. The stages of the APL process are shown below:

- Recruitment
- Computer system familiarisation
- Autobiographical Account (CV)
- Portfolio Composition of claims and accompanying evidence
- Counselling and Initial Assessment
- Top-up (where necessary) to required NVQ
- Internal Validation
- External moderation

Recruitment

The initial staff contact with the prospective candidate is usually a preliminary informal chat to explain the process and to talk over the individual's past. At the end of this session, which during the project has lasted anything from half-an-hour to three hours and has taken place in staffrooms, at the work place and in one memorable case, in the college car park, there is a preliminary decision by the candidate as to whether the scheme is for him or her. The staff counsellor will also make a professional judgement as to the extent and depth of the individual's experience.

This judgement by the member of staff cannot be made at this stage wholly on quantifiable data; the nature of the process is such that the amount and suitability of evidence is only available for assessment later in the APL process. There must be a preliminary assessment by a professional tutor not only of the candidate's experience but also of his or her likely ability to handle the demands of the APL route. There is no doubt that while we have candidate support as one of the top priorities, a great deal of the process is the individual's own responsibility and those who are motivated and who can organise their own work will find APL, and subsequent tutor support self-study, easier to deal with.

If after initial screening the student appears to be able to benefit from APL, a welcome pack explaining the operation of the Crosskeys and Newport APL route in detail is issued, together with a proforma for the systematic construction of a CV or, as the validating bodies call it, an autobiographical account. An appointment is then made for the next meeting with the member of the team who is counselling and assessing that individual. During the project, attendance at the second meeting has been taken as confirmation of intent, and enrolment takes place at this stage. It has been standard practice to contact those who fail to make this appointment to see if waverers can be encouraged.

The counsellor who will guide the candidate through the development of the portfolio is likely to be a generalist whose skills are in the diagnosis of competence and skill and the building up of a profile. We would hope that when numbers have increased we would be able to establish an APL workshop where individuals following a variety of qualifications could organise their portfolio construction, working at their own pace.

Computer System Familiarisation
The second stage of the process is to introduce the computer system to the individual candidates. The APL process is based on individual experiences which differ in nature and extent. To keep operating costs realistic the core process of refining each individual's experience into particular elements of competence and associated performance criteria will be achieved through a computer-based system of prompt questions. The competences which are claimed are matched against the NVQ assessment standards. An initial assessment of the validity of claims is also based on the candidate's record detailing how recent the experience has been, its depth and frequency. Multi-choice testing routines have been built into the assessment process.

Autobiographical Account
When the system is fully developed, a print-out will be obtained, matching the individual's claims against the requirements of the NVQ and providing a top-up learning programme to bring the individual up to the requirements of the full qualification. The

questioning process will enable the counsellor to assess the strength of the claims, singling out those that seem the most suspect.

Portfolio Composition
Working with guidance, the individual will begin to collate evidence that can support the claims of competence. Experience has shown that there is a tendency for this phase of the process to move towards one-to-one staff-candidate contact. Individuals are keen to prove their competence but there are very real problems in accepting evidence.

Guidelines from the validating bodies state that the evidence must be: valid; reliable; authentic; cost effective; efficient; accessible. The main types of indirect evidence can be classified as: chronological accounts of competence, physical products of work experience; photographs of episodes of experience and previous accreditation, other supporting documentation (including references).

Counselling and Initial Assessment
With all indirect evidence there are problems of validity and authenticity. It has been our policy to back up this form of evidence with interviews or similar checking procedures. We have encountered problems with candidates who do not want their employers approached or who cannot get information related to past work because their companies have closed (this is a particulr problem for people employed by heavy engineering firms in the early 1980s). Many certificates produced to validate claims are in fact generalised documents of overall suitability, rather than particular competences, or are often certificates of course attendance and completion (not skill acquisition). One aspect of evidence evaluation that leads to deep water is the need to differentiate between the professionalism of different employers. We are aware that this is a factor and have taken steps to develop rigorous supporting interview/assessment procedures.

An associated problem is that many of the testimonials are written by the lay public who have little idea of the specificity and terminology of competence training. Staff on the project have also found credit transfer and equivalence, particularly in regard to Armed Service certification and in-company training courses, very difficult to work through. This was a particular problem for one of our candidates who learnt mostly by experience as a member of a tank crew with the Army. It is interesting that in the USA considerable work has been carried out to allow military awards a civilian equivalence.

As a final dose of salt to rub into the experience/authenticity wound, one of our candidates works with her husband, managing a steak house and he is the principal referee; as a matter of policy, evidence from close family is not acceptable. Many of these problems can be exacerbated when evidence is gained in activities outside organised work, eg in the black economy, community work and family life.

All these problems with indirect evidence lead both counsellor and candidate to look towards further work-based assessment. While this is sustainable during the project period it will have to be minimised when APL becomes another part of mainstream delivery. The cost of the time taken to organise and operate the assessment, and the cost and time of travel if workplace assessment is necessary, can be prohibitive. Our APL tutors agree that we should make great efforts to use and authenticate secondary evidence whenever possible.

In fact, like other forms of flexible delivery APL begins to stress the importance of time management for the individual. To many tutors it is alien to their concept of responsibility to limit contact time, but if APL is to be cost-comparable then staff increasingly are realising that they must organise APL-based delivery within economic restraints.

Top-up Programme

At the end of this stage the candidate will have drawn up a list of claimed competences, achieved in a specified environment, accompanied by evidence. A top-up programme will then be drawn up. We realise that the ultimate success of the APL system is dependent on the flexibility of top-up/refresher training; it is pointless to enable an individual to claim a part NVQ as quickly and efficiently as possible if the required top-up is still offered within a conventional framework. At present top-up is offered through a mixture of open learning, in-fill and directed work experience (which itself becomes part of APL). The two colleges are also developing a modularisation exemplar project based initially on the BTEC National Level General Engineering Diploma. We believe that the APL pilot is the key to a general unlocking of the FE system and that as the need for continual adult updating begins to dictate changes in provision, the delivery of top-up will become easier to manage.

Internal Validation

The assessor who has worked through the development of the portfolio with the candidate will have regularly checked progress. When both parties are satisfied with the portfolio the candidate will pass through to the internal validation stage. Internal validation will be completed by a different member of staff from the counsellor. The portfolio itself will be prefaced by the CV and will contain a matrix record of unit accreditation. There will also be a record of individual incidences of evidence.

The validator will be a subject specialist who will analyse the portfolio, which contains evidence of successful completion of the top-up programme, and question the candidate. The validator may well feel it necessary to ask the candidate to demonstrate some of the claimed competences.

External Moderation

As with all types of assessment, external moderation plays an essential quality assurance role. As such, both the process itself and evidence collected via APL are open to the scrutiny of the awarding bodies. The awarding bodies involved in the pilot scheme developed guidelines to help colleges prepare for this aspect of APL.

Embedding APL

The Training Agency NCVQ national APL feasibility study ended in December 1989. During the project we have examined ways of embedding the skills, techniques and processes of APL into mainstream post-16 training. Gwent LEA has given a commitment to seek support to continue the project and the team is confident of continuing to attract candidates in viable numbers.

Our belief in APL has been confirmed by the interest shown in our work by other FE institutions. Project staff have made inputs into a number of outside prestigious staff training events. In the autumn of 1989 we worked with the Welsh Joint Education Committee (WJEC) to provide two training days, one in North Wales, the other in the South. It has become apparent that we are developing particular expertise, especially in counselling, portfolio preparation and assessment.

If APL is to become a cost-effective training resource then the most effective method of delivery will be through an open access workshop which will act as a base and advice centre for candidates preparing portfolios. This would be multi-disciplinary and would provide a cohort group of an acceptable size.

As regards individual tutor skills, we went into the project with an assumption that there would be generalists and specialists operating at different stages of the project. While we are committed to a final assessment stage led by a specialist, we have found that many of our subject specialists have considerable skills in leading individuals through the task of preparing a portfolio. Generally the project team has not ventured down the road of specialist personal counselling; we see the APL counsellor's role to be more akin to that of the subject/ personal tutor who provides professional support.

In the preparation of portfolios, much work has been completed in offering guidelines for candidates. Much of the integrity of the quality of the evidence relies upon the honesty and accuracy of the endorser; to this end we have developed specimen letters of endorsement and proformas for authenticating specific competences. The endorsement of competence becomes more complicated in the case of some vocationally-based schemes qualifications. For example, within schemes such as Caterbase the competences must be gained in an environment where commercial factors such as time and scale of operation are important. Here the environment in which the competence is gained becomes more important and this creates problems of validation within APL. In contrast, within City and Guilds awards, evidence from a variety of contexts outside the commercial work place can be drawn on.

THE CASE FOR MAINSTREAM PROVISION

The APL and open learning top-up delivery system is student-centred, but is expensive in terms of hardware and tutorial time. One-to-one staff counselling time is essential initially to reassure often-insecure APL students and to encourage them to produce full past experience portfolios. During our project, a different member of staff then checked and assessed the validity of the student's APL claims.

An individual learning schedule to top-up each student to a full qualification as part of an NVQ must be negotiated to cover those competences that need updating or acquiring from scratch. Flexible delivery of these individual student learning plans must then follow. Finally, assessment of the newly-acquired topped-up competences against NVQ performance criteria must be planned and eventually undertaken by the same second member of staff who originally assessed the validity of that student's APL portfolio claims. These APL learning and assessment processes may be managed by a combination of work-based and college-based provision, assisted by computer-based delivery to standardise and economise wherever possible.

It is unlikely that the above processes will ever be cheaper than traditional group tuition. However the initial user-friendly individual counselling, no boring repetition of learning already achieved, self-paced and negotiated learning schedules, the opportunity to begin at any time of the year and the opportunity to complete an NVQ more quickly than under traditional time-serving group delivery, are all clear quality benefits of the APL delivery system. Thus given that we need to provide an attractive service – especially to the mature student – APL may allow for a more effective use of resources.

For APL to become a mainstream FE delivery system, innovative arrangments will need to be agreed between colleges and their LEAs for funding the process. These arrangements must be fully compatible with the new college financing systems that will be phased in over the next three or four years as required by the Education Reform Act. Two arrangements are essential if APL delivery is to be incorporated into general FE provision:

1 APL students should pay only the same subsidised LEA tuition fee recommended for students receiving the qualification in traditional groups of normal time-served length. (These subsidised fees are forecast to rise quite sharply to around 40 per cent of full cost over the next three to four years from, for example, the current 12 per cent in Gwent.) Obviously special fees at higher levels would continue to be charged for customised provision for single organisations. Full-cost recovery of delivery costs however for all APL students would severely restrict APL open access for self-sponsored students, particularly those who are unemployed, unwaged or in low-paid jobs.

2 Colleges must receive full LEA funding for individual APL students equal to that allocated for individual students taking the same qualification under group tuition for a traditional time-served course length. This arrangement will provide realistic costing parameters within which to fund APL delivery at costs that match existing provision. It will enable colleges to replace without financial penalty the decreasing number of 16 to 19-year-old students with an equal number of adult APL students.

Neither of the above arrangements would increase costs of provision for the LEA or worsen college efficiency. Our proposed method for costing APL delivery into mainstream FE requires the calculation of the APL student caseload necessary to justify the full cost of a full-time member of college staff. Our calculations are based on the current Gwent LEA proposed formulae for post Education Reform Act financing of FE colleges. These formulae will vary between different LEAs according to policy at local level and may be further renegotiated within Gwent.

An economic APL-based delivery system will develop using an effective computer-managed system. This, when fully developed, will simplify the process for both candidates and tutor. Related work using artificial intelligence systems to allow competence-based accreditation, carried out for the Training Agency as part of ET assessment, has shown that a computer-based approach has great potential. Contrary to some earlier views, individual mature students of all abilities seem quite keen to use computers and the structured approach of the system makes the APL process more accessible to individuals. We are also interested in exploring the potential of linking the APL system with computer-based training programmes that would form the basis of at least part of subsequent top-up training. This will require the APL system to specify a training menu possibly incorporating interactive video.

At present our APl management system has been developed using D BASE 3+ routines. However, we intend to move towards the development of an expert system shell prototype which will enable the development of a more sophisticated and faster system. The two colleges have received support from the Training Agency to carry forward this consultant-supported developmental work.

List of abbreviations

APL –	Accreditation of Prior Learning
BGT –	Business Growth Training
BTEC –	Business and Technician Education Council
CBI –	Confederation of British Industry
C&G –	City and Guilds of London Institute
CITB –	Construction Industry Training Board
CPVE –	Certificate of Pre-Vocational Education
DE –	Department of Employment
DES –	Department of Education and Science
ECCTIS –	Educational Counselling and Credit Transfer Information Service
EITB –	Engineering Industry Training Board
ERA –	Education Reform Act
ET –	Employment Training
FE –	Further Education
FESC –	Further Education Staff College
FEU –	Further Education Unit
Generic Units	units based on fundamental aspects of competence and common occupational activities: similar to CBI's common learning outcomes and DES' core skills
HE –	Higher Education
LEA –	Local Education Authority
LIB –	Lead Industry Body – industry standard settings bodies
NCC –	National Curriculum Council
NCVQ –	National Council for Vocational Qualifications
NROVA –	National Record of Vocational Achievement
NSTO –	Non-Statutory Training Organisation
NTI –	A New Training Initiative
NVQ –	National Vocational Qualification
OU –	Open University
PICKUP –	Professional Industrial and Commercial Updating Programme

RAC –   Regional Advisory Council
RCB –   Regional Curriculum Base
RSA –   Royal Society of Arts Examining Board
RVQ –   Review of Vocational Qualifications
SEAC –   Secondary Education and Assessment Council
SL –   Senior Lecturer
S/SR –   Staff/Student Ratio
TA –   Training Agency, Department of Employment
                 (previously TC – Training Commission, pre-
                 viously MSC – Manpower Services Commission)
TAPS –   Training Access Points database
TEC –   Training and Enterprise Council
TVEI –   Technical and Vocational Education Initiative
VET –   Vocational Education and Training
WJEC –   Welsh Joint Education Committee
WRNAFE –   Work-Related Non Advanced Further Education
YT(S) –   Youth Training (Schemes)

Index